English on the Internet 1999–2000:

A Prentice Hall Guide

English
on the Internet
1999–2000:
A Prentice Hall Guide

Andrew T. Stull

Adapted for English by
Emily Thiroux
University of Baltimore

Prentice Hall, *Upper Saddle River, NJ 07458*

ISBN 0-13-022073-6

TRADEMARK INFORMATION:
America Online is a registered trademark of America Online, Inc.;
CompuServe is a registered trademark of CompuServe, Incorporated;
Microsoft Windows is a trademark of Microsoft Corporation;
Mosaic is copyrighted by the Board of Trustees of the University of Illinois (UI);
Netscape Navigator is a registered trademark of Netscape Communications Corporation;
JavaScript is a registered trademark of Sun Microsystems;
Internet Explorer is a registered trademark of Microsoft Corporation.

The authors and publisher of this manual have used their best efforts in preparing this book. The authors and publisher make no warranty of any kind, expressed or implied, with regard to these programs or the documentation contained in this book. The author and publisher shall not be liable in any event for incidental or consequential damages in connection with, or arising out of, the furnishing, performance, or use of the programs described in this book.

Contents

Preface   Change!   vii

Introduction   O' Brave New World: Brief
Internet History   ix

Chapter 1   What Makes It Tick? The Basics   1

1.1   Springs, wheels, and dials—Connecting   2
1.2   Putting the pieces together—Organizing   7
Activity: *The Starting Line*   10

Chapter 2   Hitting the Road: Mapping the Net   12

2.1   Cruising the Net—Browsing   12
2.2   Landmarks—Navigating   16
2.3   Asking for directions—Searching   21
Activity: *The Great Cybertrip*   26

Chapter 3   Traveling in Style: As You Like It   28

3.1   Coffee, tea, or milk?—Customizing   28
3.2   Wish you were here—Communicating   37
3.3   The fun is in the going—Extending   49
Activity: *A Talkabout Tour*   53

Chapter 4   A Unique Online Study Resource:
The Companion Website™   54

4.1   Locating Companion Websites   54

4.2 Getting Started 56
4.3 Navigation 62
4.4 The Modules 63

Appendix I Internet Resources for English 79

Appendix II Documenting Your Electronic Sources 93

Appendix III Evaluating Online Sources 98

Glossary Fasten Your Seatbelts: Jargon to Go 100

Preface
Change!

The artist picks up the message of cultural and technological challenge decades before its transforming impact occurs. *

Change! The original edition of this manual gasped its first breath at 7:22 p.m. on July 23, 1995. Since then, a great deal about the World Wide Web and the world at large has changed. Our world is louder, faster, and more complex than the one experienced by earlier generations. In terms of information transfer, we might be described as a techno-generation; our parents, as a paper-generation. The World Wide Web has changed as well, and it will probably continue to do so; our online future is likely to be chaotic but exciting. Prepare to revel in the difference that tomorrow will bring.

Reading this manual won't teach you all there is to know about the World Wide Web, but it will help you to teach yourself. In the future you will need to find information for yourself rather than relying solely on others, who may bear outdated knowledge. If you are successful, your skills in "cruising" the Internet will allow you to deal with ongoing change. By the end of this manual, you should be comfortable and resourceful in navigating the complexity of the Internet, from its back eddies to its thriving thoroughfares.

This manual has four chapters. In the Introduction, *O' Brave New World*, we will describe the origin of and the innovations behind the Internet. In Chapter 1, *What Makes It Tick?*, we will explain the use of a Web browser and describe how you can connect to the Internet. The boxed and end-of-chapter exercises will give you practice in using your browser as well as introduce you to some of the wonderful places on the Internet.

*After each major heading, you'll see a quote from *Understanding Media, The Extensions of Man* (MIT Press, Cambridge, MA, 1964) by Marshall McLuhan. See also "McLuhan Meets the Net," by Larry Press, Communications of the ACM, July 1995.

In Chapter Two, *Hitting the Road*, you'll learn more about how to use your browser in order to cruise the endless byways of the Internet. Also, you will be introduced to resources and strategies for information searching. The boxed and end-of-chapter exercises will reinforce your navigational skills and give you practice in searching for some of the great English and English-related sites on the Internet. These resources, along with related newsgroups, appear in Appendix I.

In Chapter Three, *Traveling in Style*, you will learn how to customize your Web browser to make it more responsive to your needs. You will find yourself changing from an observer into an enthusiastic Internet participant. The boxed and end-of-chapter exercises will help you contact others on the Internet.

In Chapter Four, *A Unique Online Study Resource*, you will learn about an additional Web resource that is available with many Prentice Hall books. The text-specific websites allow you to take practice tests, to link directly with other websites relating to the topic being studied, and to share ideas with others studying the same subject.

Internet resources are listed in Appendix I, and Appendices II and III discuss documenting and evaluating online sources. Finally, a glossary defines the buzzwords.

Introduction
O' Brave New World
Brief Internet History

As electrically constructed, the globe is no more than a village.

This thing that we now call the Internet has been evolving ever since it was first developed over twenty-five years ago. Many people have compared the Internet to a living creature because of the way it grows and changes. You may find its history quite interesting.

In the late 1950s and early 1960s, scientists and engineers realized the importance of sharing information and communicating through their computers. Many different groups attempted to develop computer network languages that would enable computers to exchange information with one another. But unfortunately, all of these computer systems used different languages—people on different systems still had difficulty communicating with one another. It was like the Tower of Babel all over again.

The Internet was born as the solution to this problem. The U.S. government paid for the development of a common network language, called a protocol, which was eventually shared freely. Over time, many formerly isolated networks from all over the world adopted this language. Thus, the best description of the Internet is that it is not a network, but a network of networks. However, the Internet is independent of governments and regulation—there is no central Internet agency. Change is spurred by the common needs of the people that use the Internet.

Admittedly, this type of network system isn't the most graceful—but it works. If you saw a diagram of this great big computer network, you might find it resembles a spider's web. On this web, information can travel between any two points along any one of many possible paths.

Originally, the chief purpose of the Internet was to provide a distribution system for scientific exchange and research. Gradually, however, the Internet also became a digital post office, enabling people to send mail and transfer computer files electronically. Although the Internet is still used extensively by scientists, the commercial sector is currently the most powerful force behind its growth.

As technology changed, the speed with which information could be transferred and the way we viewed information changed. In 1991, an important new user interface was developed at the University of Minnesota: the *Gopher*. *Gopher* is a visually-oriented search tool for the Internet that allows users to locate information found on other computers. Because of *Gopher*, and other, more sophisticated *graphical user interfaces* developed since 1991, it is now possible to search through vast stores of information on computers all over the world. Once the desired information is found, it can be easily downloaded to the user's computer. Amazing if you think about it! You could be on your computer in Shepherdstown, West Virginia, and view information from London, Mexico City, or Tokyo without even realizing it. Wham! And no airline tickets!

In 1992, researchers in Switzerland helped to create a new format for information exchange that led to the explosive growth of the World Wide Web (WWW). Information on the Web is posted as a "page" that may contain text, images, sounds, and even movies. The organization of a page is much like any printed page in a book. However, Web pages make use of *hypermedia*. Hypermedia involves the use of words and images as links, or connecting points, between different texts, images, sounds, or movies on other computers throughout the world. *Hypertext* Web pages contain links only to other text documents.

However, the introduction of the Web created a dilemma: It was a great place to go, but there was no easy way to get there. We still lacked a convenient software program that would allow users to access the Web easily. In 1993, a program called *Mosaic* was developed by the National Center for Supercomputing Applications (NCSA). It allowed the user to browse Web pages as well as use other Internet resources such as electronic mail (e-mail).

In 1991, around 700,000 people were using the Internet. After the introduction of *Mosaic*, users increased to around 1.7 million. Upon the release of Netscape *Navigator*, users were estimated at 3.2 million. Since then, the growth hasn't slowed much—various estimates suggest that the number of people who have access to the Internet ranges from 20 million to 100 million.

Just listen to the popular media. When was the last time you saw a television program, heard a radio commercial, or read a magazine without encountering something about the Internet? Today, you have access to animation, video clips, audio files, and even virtual reality worlds. Imagine all the new ways we will be able to view tomorrow's digital world.

For those of you who already have some Web experience, here are a few Web addresses discussing the history and growth of the Internet. Simply type the address into your Web browser exactly as it appears below. If you are just beginning to learn about the Internet, you might want to visit these sites after you learn more about Web browsers and Internet addresses in Chapter 2.

BBN Timeline
BBN includes an Internet history timeline. It places the important Internet events in context with other historical events and throws in plenty of social commentary to give you perspective.
Address: http://www.bbn.com/timeline/

Hobbes' Internet Timeline
Hobbes' site offers a great deal about the Internet, the people who use it, and online culture.
Address: http://info.isoc.org/guest/zakon/Internet/History/HIT.html

Netizens: On the History and Impact of Usenet and the Internet
This is a comprehensive collection of essays about the history, nature, and impact of the Internet.
Address: http://www.columbia.edu/~hauben/netbook/

English on the Internet 1999–2000:

A Prentice Hall Guide

Chapter 1
What Makes It Tick?
The Basics

An Indian is the servomechanism of his canoe,
as the cowboy of his horse or the executive of his clock.

Many of you reading this manual have a lot of experience with computers, while others have little or none. In the first section of this chapter, we will briefly describe the basic computer setup you'll need, how to use a modem, and choose an Internet Service Provider (ISP). Many of you may have computers on your campus that are set up to allow Internet access. In case you don't, we'll list the minimum in terms of systems, connections, and services that you'll need for the Internet.

In the second section of this chapter, we will explain some of the idiosyncrasies of the Internet and describe the general features of most Internet browser software. A popular Web browser, Netscape *Navigator* or *Communicator*, is used to illustrate discussions. Another popular browser is Microsoft *Internet Explorer*. We will refer to the 4.0 version of both browsers; they are the two clear frontrunners in user popularity. However, as of March 18, 1999, Microsoft announced the release of its 5.0 version of *Internet Explorer*; *Navigator* is sure to respond with its own updated version soon enough. But as of now the 4.0 versions are stable, widely accepted, and *free* to students. We don't advocate any particular browser; you will probably want to try various browsers and make up your own mind. Although our illustrations focus on *Navigator*, fear not; browsers share many of the same features. When necessary, we will point out the particulars of *Internet Explorer*. We are going to describe the features of both browsers as they pertain to the PC versions. The Macintosh versions of *Navigator* and of *Internet Explorer* have slightly different menus and layouts, but once you've learned the basic techniques, it's easy to switch back and forth between browsers and platforms.

Section 1.1
Springs, wheels, and dials—Connecting

What is the difference between a Rolex and a Timex? Without much consideration, the main difference is the price. But if we consider how well each of these watches meets our basic need for being on time, the two watches are very similar. The same goes for computers and networks. The simple no-frills components will save you money; the high-gloss gear will transform your cash into dash and make your Internet browsing only a little more enjoyable.

To get started, you'll need a *computer*, a *modem*, an *Internet connection*, and *browser software*. The descriptions that follow will help you understand each component and its function to access the Internet.

The Computer

Be careful how you approach this issue if you ask someone for advice on which computer to buy. Many people have strong opinions about the differences between Macintosh and PC-compatible systems. The best advice that we can give to you is to test them both at a computer store. Choose the one that you can pay for and are most comfortable using.

These are the *minimum* system configurations that you'll need:

PC-Compatible
- Intel 486
- Windows 3.1
- VGA monitor
- 16 MB of RAM
- 8 MB of free disk space for browser software

Macintosh
- 68030
- MacOS 7.0
- 256 color monitor
- 16 MB of RAM
- 8 MB of free disk space for browser software

If you are purchasing a new computer, the minimum may not be readily available and therefore is not recommended. Stepping up to a Power-Mac (with MacOS 7.6 or higher) or a Pentium-based PC (with Windows 9x) would be more desirable.

A new innovation is the Network Computer, or NC. An NC is a computer without all of the software that you expect in an ordinary computer: word processing, drawing, graphing, and number crunching. Because these features may be helpful to you, you should consider the purchase of an NC carefully. An NC (a box that sits on top of your TV) will allow you to connect your television directly to the Internet. *Web*TV is currently the most popular, but we suspect that you'll see many different brands in the future. The advantage of such products is that they are much cheaper than an ordinary (but more capable) computer. Also, you don't have to be a computer whiz to use them.

The Modem

You probably want to know why you need a modem if you already have a computer. A modem is a device that MOdulates and DEModulates—that is, it translates a computer signal into a telephone signal, and vice versa. Although computers and telephones were set up to speak different "languages," you can use a modem to translate between your computer and another computer across your telephone line. Modems come in different "sizes," so don't just go out and buy the cheapest one on sale. Definitely don't buy one from a garage sale unless you really know what you're doing. Because modem technology changes so quickly, older equipment may be useful only as a doorstop. The number one thing that you need to know about a modem is its speed of transmission. Modem speeds are referred to in units called baud (a bit is a basic unit of digital information and a baud is the speed of transmitting 1 bit in 1 second). At one time a modem speed of 2600 baud was considered adequate. However, the minimum speed requirements have been steadily increasing as users demand more information at faster rates. You should purchase a modem with a speed of at least 28,800 baud (28.8K baud). With a 28.8K baud modem you can expect that it will take a few seconds to transfer a typical Web page. However, keep in mind that manufacturers will continue to introduce newer and faster modems as pages become more complex and as users demand faster speeds. If you are about to purchase a modem, the standard speed as of this writing is 56k. Connect to **http://www.miningco.com** and punch in the word "modems" into the search engine for the latest on buying a new modem. (We'll talk more about search engines a bit later but this site is very useful for all types of research.)

You also need to make sure that your modem will work with your computer's operating system. Generally, this isn't a big deal, as all modems are basically the same and top manufacturers produce software for all of the major operating systems. Just remember to read the box to make sure it contains the software you need. Included with the software is an installation manual and a phone number to a help desk. If you run into trouble, don't hesitate to try both. As for which brand of modem to purchase, buy what you can afford. Your Internet Service Provider or your campus computer administrator may recommend a particular brand of modem. Take this suggestion seriously. The technicians within your ISP or campus are likely to be familiar with the recommended modem and will be able to help you if problems arise.

The word modem may also refer to a device that allows you to connect your computer or television to a service line. By the time this guide is published, you will undoubtedly hear of things called ISDN modems and cable modems. An ISDN modem is a classic misnomer because the ISDN signal is already understood by computers and isn't modulated and doesn't need to be demodulated. The cable modem refers to a box that connects between your cable TV line (not your telephone line) and your computer or television.

The Internet Connection

Your campus may already be using the Internet as a teaching and learning tool. If not, there are many resources to help you set up a connection from home.

Some campuses, although lacking a walk-in lab, have made arrangements for students to dial into the campus computer system and connect to the Internet with a modem. If this is the case, search out the campus computer guru and ask for help.

Another option is to subscribe to a company such as *America Online, CompuServe, Microsoft Network*, or one of the many independent Mom and Pop companies currently offering monthly access to the Internet. It is a buyer's market and you should shop around. Test drive everything before you buy. This will save you a great deal of frustration. Here are a few things to consider when choosing an Internet Service Provider:

> **Does the ISP have a local number for your area?** You need to call the provider each time you access the Internet. Paying a toll call every time you do so will become costly if you use the Internet regularly.
> **Can their system handle a large number of simultaneous connections?** Ask them how many users they can handle at one time and how many subscribers they have. Although they may

have a reasonable price and a local number, it doesn't mean much if you can't get on to use it. If after you subscribe you find that you are never able to connect or that the only available access is late at night or early in the morning, find a new ISP.

Do they offer SLIP/PPP connections? This is the type of connection that you'll need if you want to use a graphical browser like Navigator or Internet Explorer. Some ISPs only offer shell accounts. Shell accounts require you to type in each command as you would with a command-line interface such as provided in DOS. It is somewhat like driving a horse and buggy when everyone else has an automobile.

Do they have a reasonable monthly subscription fee? Cheapest is not always best. The added features and the staffing support are important points to consider when choosing a service. Some Internet Service Providers offer you unlimited monthly connect time for a flat fee and others charge for a specific number of hours per month (with hourly rates thereafter). Estimate your expected usage and purchase accordingly. Ask if there is a fee to upgrade your service if you find that you need more time. If you have a roommate, consider upgrading the service and splitting the cost. This may save you money.

Does your ISP include the Internet browser software in the price? You'll find that not all do. Most ISPs have an agreement with either Netscape or Microsoft to bundle their browser software. The provided software may also be partially configured to work on the ISP's system. Moreover, the technicians will be better able to help you with a problem.

Is the ISP a regional or local company? This may not be important to everyone, but some of you may go home during holidays and vacations. If the ISP covers a wider area, then you can still check your e-mail and cruise the Net when you are away from school.

Do they have a help line in case you need technical assistance to set up your connection? Call the help line before you subscribe and make sure you get a real person. Although you may be asked to leave your name and number, you should expect to get a return call within 24 hours. If they don't return your call within this period, then the service is probably understaffed or poorly managed.

Does the ISP offer both newsgroup and e-mail access in addition to a connection to the Web? This is usually standard but there are always exceptions.

Does it cost you extra for additional e-mail addresses? If you have a roommate, then you may find that it is more affordable to split the cost of a subscription and pay for an additional e-mail account.

Will your ISP add newsgroups at your request? Most ISPs subscribe to a small fraction of the available newsgroups and you may find that they don't include some of the basic, academic groups that your instructors may recommend. It shouldn't cost anything for the ISP to add these groups to their list.

Does the ISP offer you space for your own Web page? Often, one of the features offered in the basic package is the option of posting your own homepage. A limited amount of memory will be provided by the ISP.

The most important thing to remember when using an ISP is to expect courteous and prompt service. If you don't like what you are paying for, then cancel and go somewhere else. There are plenty of competitors willing to offer you better service.

The Browser Software

A descriptive name for software such as *Navigator* or *Internet Explorer* is *browser* software, because that is what most people do with it. It is used to browse or wander, sometimes aimlessly, through the Internet.

Many Web browsers are on the market today, and new ones frequently enter the race to capture your dollar.

All browsers have advantages and disadvantages. You should evaluate several and choose the one that is most comfortable for you. (However, when choosing a browser, remember that seeing over the dashboard is all that is really important. Don't get wrapped up in features that you'll never use.) *Navigator, Internet Explorer,* and many of the other browsers are free for student use! Don't be afraid to look at several. At the end of the chapter you will find several Web addresses that offer such software. Of course, if you purchase the browser at the store, you also get a user's manual, which you don't get with the free, educational copy.

If you have all of these basic elements and they've been put together correctly, you should be ready to surf. (See the activity at the end of this chapter, *The Starting Line.*) The rest of this manual is devoted to guiding you through some of the wonderful places that will allow you to enjoy the depth and scope of English.

Section 1.2
Putting the pieces together—Organizing

The software that you'll use to access the Net is commonly called a *client* or a Web *browser*. It functions according to an information exchange model called the *client-server model* (Figure 1.1). In this way, a *client* (your Web browser software) communicates with a server (a computer with Web server software) on the Internet to exchange information. When referring to the Web, the information that your browser receives from the server is called a page.

What really appears on these Web pages? The best way to find out is to see for yourself. Sit down in front of a computer, start your browser software, and connect to the Internet. Your browser is probably already set to start at a specific page. This start page is often referred to as a *homepage*. Web pages usually include both text and images. Some also use sounds and videos. The use of different information types is called multimedia. A basic rule of the road is that anything that can be saved or recorded onto a computer can be distributed on the Internet through a Web page.

When you choose a page it will be sent to your computer. After the requested information has been sent by the server, your computer will display it for you. However, sometimes the Internet is not as responsive as you'd like. (Why do you think some people refer to the World Wide Web as the World Wide Wait?) A few analogies and real-world considerations may help you see why this is so.

Patchwork Quilts
The patchwork quilt you might use during cold nights is one analogy. The quilt may have been crafted by your grandmother. Or in another

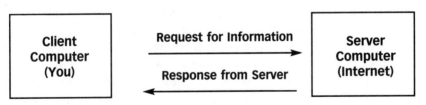

Figure 1.1. The client requests information from the server. The requested information is displayed on the client computer.

time, a community of women (not all with equal sewing talent) may have met to produce a single quilt from a collection of patches differing in color, shape, and pattern. Due to the complexity, age, use, care, and variations in craftsmanship, quilts eventually become threadbare and require mending. The Internet is just like your favorite quilt in this respect.

Spider Webs

As we mentioned in the introduction, the Internet can be thought of as a big spider web. If you're the spider and you're trying to get to a fly stuck in the web, you usually have more than one path to get there. Some paths are more direct than others, but there are choices. Like a spider web, sometimes a small section of the Internet drops out of the "Web" and traffic has to be rerouted. This obviously causes increased traffic on the remaining strands, which in turn increases your waiting time.

Far Away Places

Remember that the Internet mimics the real world. Distance is a factor in determining how long it takes to access a Web page. Generally, loading a page from a machine across town is much faster than loading a page from across the nation or across the world.

Time Zones and Lunch

The world works on different time zones and the Internet does too. And what about lunch? Most people in the Western world take lunch around noon, and many of them check their e-mail or browse the Web as well. You can usually expect Internet traffic to be slow during that time. Let's now consider the distance factor. There is a three-hour time difference between the East and West coasts of North America, so the lunch rush lasts about four hours. Your location will determine if you are on the lead, middle, or tail end of the rush. Plan accordingly.

Parking Lots

Surfing the Web can be like shopping during the holidays. You either arrive early or park a few miles away. Here's the connection: A transaction occurs between your computer and another when you load a Web page for viewing. You require a document (a Web page) from somewhere on the Internet (a server). Obviously, a slow connection to the Internet on the client side may cause delays. But consider what is happening on the server end of the transaction. Small, slow servers will take longer to serve Web pages than large, fast servers. Now think about the holiday rush: Although there is normally adequate parking, a holiday sale and a limited number of parking spaces can add hours to your shopping. It should not be difficult to see how large, fast servers can be rapidly overloaded if they are hosting a really interesting Web site.

When Microsoft released an updated version of Internet Explorer, over twenty state-of-the-art machines went down because of excessive demand. Basically, Microsoft's parking lot wasn't big enough for the shopping rush.

By this time, you probably understand enough about each of the basic components of an Internet to try it out. Even if you're feeling unsure, don't worry. You don't need to know everything there is to know about each component. And you can always learn more from the user's guides provided by the manufacturers. Just take it one step at a time and you'll piece everything together.

Activity:
The Starting Line

There's no better time than now to get started. And you really don't need a destination to have fun. This activity is intended to help you get ready to cruise or surf the Internet. Even if you don't have a computer to access the Internet, use a friend's computer or one on campus to view this material.

The Browser
You should have a computer and a modem. Use the following Internet addresses to research the right browser for you.

>**Netscape**
>>http://www.netscape.com
>
>**Microsoft**
>>http://www.microsoft.com
>
>**Browserwatch**
>>http://browserwatch.internet.com

The Internet Service Provider
With your computer, modem, *and* browser, you're only one step away. Use the following Internet addresses to research the right ISP for you.

>**Choosing the Internet Service Provider (Netscape)**
>>http://home.netscape.com/assist/isp_select/index.html
>
>**Internet Access Provider Guide**
>>http://www.liii.com/~dhjordan/students/docs/welcome.htm
>
>**Choosing An Internet Provider**
>>http://tcp.ca/Dec95/Commtalk_ToC.html
>
>**Internet Service Providers by Area Code**
>>http://thelist.internet.com

Research
It's always nice to have an independent opinion; therefore, read what the critics have to say. The following Internet addresses are for two of the largest publishers of computer-related magazines. Between them, they

print nearly 50 different popular periodicals about computers and the Internet. Search their databases for articles that will help you make Internet decisions. You can read the articles online.

CMP Media (Publisher of *Windows Magazine* and others)
http://www.techweb.com/info/publications/publications.html
Ziff Davis (Publisher of *PC Magazine*, *MacWEEK*, and others)
http://www5.zdnet.com/findit/search.html

Chapter 2
Hitting the Road
Mapping the Net

*Under electronic technology the entire business of man
becomes learning and knowing.*

By now, you should be prepared to see the world, or at least the World
Wide Web. In this chapter, you'll develop a better understanding of the
browser as a tool for navigating the Internet. The first section discusses
basic navigation techniques; the second describes how to read Internet
addresses; and the third introduces you to some of the information tools
available on the Internet for finding your way around.

Section 2.1
Cruising the Net—Browsing

Even though the Internet is vast, finding your way around is no harder
than finding your way to a friend's house. Information on the Internet has
an address just as your friends do. Most browsers allow you to type in an
address and thereby access information, or "go to" a particular document.

The two most common browsers are Netscape *Navigator* and
Microsoft *Explorer*. Let's take a look at how to enter an address using the
Web browser Netscape *Navigator*, shown in Figure 2.1. Start by finding the
text entry box, which is located to the right of the word *Location*. (Some-
times the word *Netsite* or *Address* is used instead.) If you have *Navigator* (or
Explorer), type in the address and press the return button on your keyboard.

Now take a look at the row of boxes directly above the text box. Each
one contains an icon; together, they are known as the *tool bar*. Clicking on
an individual box causes the computer to execute the command in the box.

How do each of these commands help you navigate the Internet?
Let's return to our analogy. Suppose you go to a friend's new home for a
party but forget the house-warming present. What do you do? Drive

home, of course. A Web browser will let you do something similar. In Figure 2.1, find the button labeled *Back*—it's at the far left. By clicking on this button you can return to the Web page you just visited. If you have gone to many Web pages, you can use it repeatedly to make your way back to your starting point.

Here's the address of a site you might want to visit. The Associated Press and *US News and World Report* provide free news services. You can reach them at the following addresses:

http://wire.ap.org

http://www.usnews.com/usnews/home.htm

Now find the *Home* button. By selecting this button, you will immediately return to the homepage configured for your browser. When you first begin using your browser, it will be set to a page determined by the company that created it.

Two other buttons common to most browsers are *Stop* and *Reload* (this button is called *Refresh* in *Explorer*). *Stop* is pretty easy to understand but *Reload/Refresh* needs just a bit more explanation. As you explore more of the Internet, you'll realize that complete pages don't show up in your browser window instantly. Instead, different types of elements (pictures, icons, text, animations, etc.) appear over time as they are moved from the server to your browser. Occasionally, you'll notice that a page loads without some of these elements. This is often caused by an error in the transmission. Use the *Reload/Refresh* button to request a new copy of the page.

You don't always have to know the address of a page to view it. The wonderful thing about the Web is that you can access pages through the

Figure 2.1. The tool bar for Netscape *Navigator* offers basic navigation features such as *Back, Forward*, and *Home*. You will find everything you'll need to navigate around the Internet.

use of hyperlinks. You will notice that hyperlinks are often colored (typically blue) and underlined words on a Web page. Images may also be hyperlinks. Your mouse is used to select or click on the desired hyperlink. Some Web authors write their pages so that their hyperlinks are hidden from you. If you aren't sure where the hyperlinks are, just click on everything. You can't break anything. Clicking on a hyperlink will take you to a new Web page just as typing in an address does.

Here are a few more places you might find both fun and interesting.

The Academy of American Poets
http://www.he.net/~susannah/academy.htm

The Shakespeare Web
http://www.shakespeare.com/

Resources for Writers and Writing Instructors
http://www.english.upenn.edu/~jlynch/writing.html

MLA Style
http://www.mla.org/main_stl.htm

Inkspot
http://www.inkspot.com/

The Bulwer-Lytton Fiction Contest
http://www.bulwer-lytton.com/

Experiment with each of the tool bar buttons on your browser. Remember that you can always use your *Back, Forward,* or *Home* buttons to retrace your steps.

The author of a Web page can connect *one* image to *many* different places. This type of hyperlink is sometimes called a *clickable map*. For example, think of a Web page with a map of an archaeological dig. The creator of such a document could place a hyperlink at various locations on the map so that your selection of these locations would take you to different information about the artifacts that were found there. For a little experience in using this type of navigation, visit the sites in the following box.

Here are three addresses that use clickable maps. They are also good places to find helpful information on sociological topics.

Atlantic Unbound: Books and Authors
http://www.theatlantic.com/atlantic/atlweb/bookauth/baindex.htm

Poetry Magazine
http://www.poetrychicago.com/

Bookwire
http://www.bookwire.com/homepage.html

Not all browsers support clickable maps. Most experienced Web authors, however, provide conventional hyperlinks to related sites in addition to the clickable map.

Some Web pages contain *forms*. A form is generally a request for information, which you may respond to by clicking with your mouse or typing an answer. Forms can be used to survey users, answer questions, or make requests. As the box below shows, you can obtain valuable information from companies, government agencies, or educational institutions.

Experiment with the following links which involve forms. Not all browsers support forms, so you will need to determine if yours does. However, if you are using the 4.0 or higher versions of *Navigator* or *Explorer*, you should be fine.

Burning Bush Publications
http://www2.cruzio.com/~abbyb/

Inkspot Feedback
http://www.inkspot.com/admin/feedback.html

Mail Your Paper to OWL
http://www.lsa.umich.edu/ecb/OWL/mailform.html

ArchiPlex Forms
http://cuiwww.unige.ch/archieplexform.html

PursuitNet Resume
http://www.tiac.net/users/jobs/eres.htm

Section 2.2
Landmarks—Navigating

The Internet addresses that you've been using are also called *Uniform Resource Locators*, or *URLs*. Each URL (pronounced "earl") has a couple of basic parts just like a residential address. Look at some of the URLs that you've used already. Do you notice any similarities among them?

Here is another typical URL (this will take you to a pretty cool site). The three basic components of an URL are listed below the address. Compare this one to the others you've seen so far.

http://www.prenhall.com/books/hss_0137592264.html

protocol	http://
server	www.prenhall.com
path	/books/hss_0137592264.html

You may notice that some addresses don't have a path element—this information is not always necessary. Be careful when you type an URL. Even one incorrect letter will prevent the browser from finding the desired site. Here is an additional resource if you'd like to learn more about Internet addresses:

http://www.ncsa.uiuc.edu/demoweb/url-primer.html

Now pick up any recent magazine and leaf through the articles and advertisements. With little effort you should be able to recognize a few more URLs. Just as you might recognize a string of numbers to be a phone number (e.g., 555-1212), you should be able to spot URLs by their characteristic form and order. An URL may seem confusing at first glance, but think of it as a postal address strung together without any spaces.

The *protocol* of the URL indicates how the information is stored. In the last box, http refers to the protocol, or language, that is used by all Web servers. The colon and slashes are used to separate it from the name of the server. They are not necessarily present in every type of URL. The *path* describes the location of the Web page on the server.

Up to this point, we have only been discussing browsers as way of navigating through information using hyperlinks. However, browsers also have the power to link to other, much older, formats of information. Try the following URLs to notice how the information differs. Although the Gopher sites are a dying breed on the Internet, you can still search for such sites at: **http://galaxy.einet.net/GJ/ index.html**. Examples of such formats are as follows:

ftp://mapping.usgs.gov/pub/ti/DEM/demguide/

gopher://liberty.uc.wlu.edu/11/library/human

HTTP, FTP, and Gopher are not the only protocols, but they are the three you're most likely to encounter. Have you ever encountered the following Internet protocols?

telnet://

wais://

news:

A domain is just a fancy name for a functional network group. The last part of the server name defines the domain to which the server belongs. The most common domain is indicated by the letters edu; all educational institutions are members of this domain group. Another important domain is com, which stands for commercial and includes Internet servers that belong to **commercial** companies. You are also likely to encounter domains that serve other groups; abbreviations for a few of these are shown below.

Here are some URLs that may help expand your understanding of domains. Can you determine what each domain group represents?

http://arts.endow.gov/

http://www.dtic.mil/

http://www.writer.org/

http://www.internic.net

http://www.en.utexas.edu/depts/engl/index.html

The first address suggests that surfing can be quite unpredictable. Don't say we didn't warn you.

In your travels, you will eventually jump to a server that is outside your country. Much, but not all, of the information on these servers is in English. URLs of servers outside the United States have an additional section at the end of the server name. It is a two letter code that indicates the country. Here are just a few examples of the many you might find. (All the country codes are listed in **http://www.ics.uci.edu/pub/ websoft/wwwstat/country-codes.txt**)

- .au   Australia
- .ca   Canada
- .ch   Switzerland
- .nl   Netherlands
- .lt   Lithuania
- .pe   Peru
- .uk   United Kingdom

Here is yet another opportunity to encounter new places on the Web. It is a directory that allows you to search for specific things. This group of tools is discussed later in the chapter, but you might want to play with it first.

Yahoo!
http://www.yahoo.com

Remember that you won't break anything. If you get lost, you can always shut down the program, have lunch, and try again later!

Return Visit

Now that you've found a number of interesting pages, how do you find them again a day or a week later? Your browser provides a way to mark an intriguing site and quickly return to it.

Navigator

Navigator uses the feature called *Bookmarks* to compile a list of pages you frequently visit. Figure 2.2 will give you an idea of what this feature looks like. When you wish to return to one of these pages, you simply select it from the list by clicking on it with your mouse. You will jump directly to the site.

Here is an URL to get your collection started. Try this address: **http://www.hotwired.com**. It's a pretty interesting place: the online ver-

Figure 2.2. As pages are added to this list they will appear in the *Bookmarks* menu.

sion of Wired Magazine. Select *Add Bookmark* from the *Bookmarks* menu (see Figure 2.2) which appears either to the left of the *Location* window or under the *Communicator/Bookmarks/Add Bookmark* menu. Later on, if you use your mouse to select the *Bookmarks* menu, you'll see that *Hotwired* is just a jump away. Thus, you don't have to memorize the URL or haphazardly jump around until you find it again.

Explorer

Explorer uses a feature called *Favorites* to compile a list of pages you frequently visit. When you wish to return to one of these pages, you simply select it from the list by clicking on it with your mouse. You will jump directly to the site. Here is an URL to get your collection started. Try this address: **http://www.hotwired.com**. It's a pretty interesting place: the online version of Wired Magazine. Select *Add to Favorites. . .* from the Favorites menu. Later on, if you use your mouse to select the *Favorites* menu, you'll see that *Hotwired* is just a jump away. Thus, you don't have to memorize the URL or haphazardly jump around until you find it again.

Now that you've got the hang of it, give the following URLs a try.

The Purdue University Writing Lab
http://owl.english.purdue.edu/our-lab/introduction.html

University of Missouri Online Writery
http://www.missouri.edu/~writery/

Beginner's Arena for HTML
http://www.deltamedia.com/crest/lists/beginner/index.html

World Lecture Hall
http://www.utexas.edu/world/lecture/index.html

Writer's Block
http://www.niva.com/writblok/index.htm

RongoRongo
http://www.netaxs.com/~trance/rongo.html

Siskel and Ebert Movie Reviews
http://www.tvplex.com/BuenaVista/SiskelAndEbert

Bartlett's Familiar Quotations
http://www.columbia.edu/acis/bartleby/bartlett/

Electronic Postcards
http://postcards.www.media.mit.edu/postcards/

1001 Links to Articles about Fiction Writing
http://www.angelfire.com/va/storyguide/

A Guide for Writing Research Papers
http://webster.commnet.edu/mla.htm

WordBot Home Page
http://www.cs.washington.edu/homes/kgolden/wordbot.html

The Skeptic's Dictionary
http://skepdic.com/

The Oxford English Dicitonary Online
http://www.oed.com/

When you find something that you think is fun and interesting, save it or give the address to a friend.

As you begin to accumulate more sites on your list, you'll notice how cluttered and disorganized they can become. In addition to the ability to collect Web addresses, most browsers also allow you to organize them as you desire.

Navigator

The *Edit Bookmarks* option allows you to organize your Web address list. When you select this option, a small window will open; in it you can move and manipulate your list of Web addresses.

Explorer

To organize your Web address list using *Explorer,* use the option called *Organize Favorites* on the toolbar. When you select this option, a small window will open; in it you can move and manipulate your list of Web addresses.

Travel History

If you've been working along with your manual and browser at the same time, you've probably been to many places on the Web. If you want to move back and forth between your selections, you're probably using the *Forward* and *Back* buttons on the browser toolbar. But what do you do if you want to go back to some place you've visited fifteen jumps ago? Do you press the *Back* button fifteen times? Well, it works, but it's a little slow. You might want to try a new feature: It allows you to jump rapidly to any of the places you've visited along your path of travel.

Navigator

Select the *Go* menu. You'll see a list of all of the places you've visited on your journey. To jump to a site on the list, simply click/select the site with your mouse. You'll also find a similar feature called *History* under the *Communicator* menu. By selecting *History*, you'll open a new window listing the names *and* the URLs for all of the places you've visited recently. Because the list compiled under *Go* or *History* begins anew each time you start your browser, you should use *Bookmarks* when you find something interesting.

Explorer

Select the *History* button on the tool bar or on the left-hand side of the Web window. You'll see the places you've visited on your journey. To jump to a site on the list, simply click/select the site with your mouse. Although the default setting causes the list compiled under *History* to begin anew each time you start your browser, you can change that setting to keep pages in history. To do so, choose *Internet Options* from the *View* menu. A pop-up window with tabbed pages will appear. Choose the *General* tab and on the bottom you'll find a box indicating the number of days pages will be kept in history. Simply insert the number of days, click on *Apply*, then close the window, and you'll be set.

Section 2.3
Asking for directions—Searching

The Internet is full of valuable information, but it's not always easy to find what you need. A number of easy-to-use tools are available for free. With practice, these tools will help you develop your information-finding skills.

There are two types of tools that you'll use most often to search for information. These are *Directories* and *Search Engines*.

Directories

Yahoo! (**http://www.yahoo.com**) is only one of many directories that are available on the Internet, but it is the best one available for general topics. (The name *Yahoo!* is taken from Jonathan Swift's *Gulliver's Travels*, which describes a Yahoo as a crude, uncivilized, and according to one of *Yahoo!'s* founders, an interesting person.)

Yahoo! began as a simple listing of information by category, kind of like a card catalog. In the last few years, it has added the ability to search for specific information. At the top level of the directory, there are several very general categories, but as you move deeper into the directory you'll notice that the categories become more specific. To find information, you simply choose the most appropriate category at the top level and continue through each successive level until you find what you're looking for (or until you realize you're in the wrong place). It's not unusual to get lost. In such cases, just begin again and try different categories.

Suppose that you're taking an English Literature course and want to find information on a specific topic (such as writing sonnets) for a research paper. Within *Yahoo!*, notice that two of the top level categories are *Poetry* and *Shakespeare, William*. Since the *Poetry* category includes *Sonnets,* it would seem to be the most appropriate place to find information on this topic, so give it a try. Note, however, that you could also search *Elizabeth Barrett Browning, Spanish Sonnets,* or *Surreal Sonnets*. Searching for *Sonnets* under poetry, you'll get over 10 "hits" (or site matches). But if you search poetry, you will find lots of other interesting topics that you might decide to research instead of sonnets, such as *Haiku* with 76 "hits" or *Poets* with 861 "hits." Because *Yahoo!* cross-references among the categories, you'll find that several related categories will lead to the information you desire.

Much of your success in finding information using a directory like *Yahoo!* centers around your preparation for the search. Often, it is possible to find information on a topic in a category that may at first seem unrelated to your topic of interest. Let's take the example of *Women's Literature*. Are you especially interested, for example, in feminist science fiction? If so, you might search under such *Literature* subcategories as *women writers, science fiction, feminist fiction,* or *Gwyneth Jones*.

Prepare yourself for a search *before* you jump into one. In the long run, it will save you both time and frustration. Don't be afraid to try some unusual approaches in your search strategy. A good technique is to pull out your thesaurus and look up other names for the topic you're searching. Think of everything associated with your question and give each of these possibilities a try. You never know what might turn up a gold mine.

Search Engines

A more direct approach to finding information on the Web is to use a *search engine*, which is a program that runs a search while you wait for the results. Many search engines can be found on the Web. Some of Web search engines are commercial and may charge you a fee to run a search. Search engines are also available for other parts of the Internet: *Archie, Veronica,* and *Jughead* are examples of such search engines.

Alta Vista (**http://www.altavista.digital.com**) offers general and detailed searches through what Digital Equipment Corporation claims is the largest Web index. According to Alta Vista, the user can search billions of words found in millions of Web pages. In addition, you can access a full-text index of more than 13,000 newsgroups.

Excite! (**http://www.excite.com**) is very versatile because it tracks down information by searching for concepts, not just keywords. Suppose, for example, that you're interested in material on age discrimination. *Excite!* can find such information even though the source describes the phenomenon (such as bias against older people) without ever using the phrase "age discrimination." *Excite!* also provides you with a percentage of how close it "thinks" it came to providing pertinent information on your concept(s). In addition, *Excite!* has such capabilities as finding a specific news article from newsgroups by a text search.

InfoSeek Guide (**http://guide.infoseek.com**) is a search/browse service that returns both search hits and a list of topics related to your search. With each search, you get the most relevant matches, related topics to explore, and current news and views from popular magazines, TV networks, and online experts. *InfoSeek Guide* also helps you find e-mail addresses, stock quotes, company profiles, and other materials.

A frequently-used search engine is *Lycos* (**http://www.lycos.com**). It's simple to operate but, as with any search tool, it takes practice and patience to master. Take the time now to connect to *Lycos*, and we'll take it for a test run. The instructions on the opening page will tell you almost everything you need to know. To search, enter a word into the white text entry box and press the submit button. *Lycos* will refer back to its database of information and return a page of hyperlinked resources containing the word you entered. When the query results come back to you, notice that they are hyperlinks to various sites on the Internet.

Regardless of which search engine you use, remember that they are all fast but dumb. In the *Sonnets* topic, for example, you'll get hundreds of "hits" that are probably not appropriate for your research paper or class presentation. To perform an effective search, you will need to spend time before the search preparing a search strategy. When you do research using an automated tool like a search engine, you can expect many links to be unrelated to your topic. Continuous research in advanced computing will undoubtedly result in smarter search engines. Until then, the most intelligent researcher is at the keyboard. Despite some misses, you'll find that search engines are very powerful tools and will save you time in the long run.

One last comment on search engines: these tools don't directly search the Internet. They actually search a database that is derived from the Internet. Here is how it works. Initially, information robots (automated programming tools) sift and categorize information on the Internet and place it into a database. It is this database that is inspected when you use a search engine. Therefore, each search engine is only as effective as its cadre of robots that generate the database. Thus it is wise not to rely on just one search engine. Use several, because what one does not find, another might.

Here's a way to test the skills you've developed from your accumulated Internet experience. Using *Yahoo!* and *Lycos* (or any of the other search tools described in this chapter) find information on the Web related to the words given below. Compare the results with searches using the additional resources provided at the bottom of this box. The last three resources (MetaCrawler, FindSpot, and Search.com) allow you to choose from a collection of search tools.

Short Stories	Gothic literature
Censorship	Online Writing Labs (OWLs)
Viruses	Romanticism
Hypertext	Intellectual Property Rights

WebCrawler
http://www.webcrawler.com

BigFoot
http://www.bigfoot.com

HotBot
http://www.hotbot.com

Dogpile.com
http://www.dogpile.com

MetaCrawler
http://www.metacrawler.com

Findspot
http://www.findspot.com

Search.com
http://www.search.com

Activity:
The Great Cybertrip

Obtaining information on the Web is easy. It may be somewhat harder to find the *right* information, however. Discovering the correct information is still exciting and interesting, not unlike getting lost and finding your way again in an unfamiliar city. The first list is a set of some commonly-heard terms in English literature and composition. See what you can find on these topics. How have each of these terms enhanced our understanding of literature and writing?

- Ode
- Satire
- Parody
- Limerick
- Sonnet
- Epithet
- Synthesis
- Paraphrase
- Hypermedia
- Netiquette

- Comma splice
- Parallelism
- Tragedy
- Gothic
- Poetic justice
- Deconstruction
- Feminist theory
- Linguistics
- Argumentation
- Exposition

Understanding English literature often means learning about the women and men who have made significant contributions in both theory and methodology. Below is a short list of some authors from the nineteenth and twentieth centuries. Some of them will be very easy to track down while other will not. We hope you'll find both their perspectives and their lives interesting.

Your assignment, should you accept it, is to put together a brief history of the authors listed below and their important contributions. If you want more of a challenge, suggest four substitutions and explain the reasons for your choices.

- Sylvia Plath
- Edgar Allan Poe
- J. D. Salinger
- Benjamin Franklin
- Alice Walker

- Mark Twain
- Emily Dickinson
- Thomas Paine
- Noah Webster
- Nathaniel Hawthorne

- Flannery O'Conner
- John Greenleaf Whittier
- John Steinbeck
- John Grisham
- Robert Frost

- ee cummings
- Truman Capote
- Henry James
- Edith Wharton
- Edna Saint Vincent Millay

Remember to use all of the resources at your disposal. Begin with *Yahoo!* and then move to the other search engines. Check the obscure as well as the popular resources. You are also welcome to read ahead to Chapter 3, which explains how to use e-mail and newsgroups. These resources may be helpful, too.

Chapter 3
Traveling in Style
As You Like It

We shape our tools and afterwards our tools shape us.

By now you have probably wandered through some of the many resources offered on the Web. In this chapter we will cover additional techniques to make your Web experience more enjoyable and beneficial.

Section 3.1
Coffee, tea, or milk?—Customizing

On the Internet, saving time is critical if you have to use a modem and an Internet Service Provider (ISP) to cruise the Net. If you know what your browser can and cannot do, and if you configure the options for your browser so that it is most efficient for you, you will save both time and money. Try the modifications described below as you read; also, feel free to jump to the information that is most important to you.

Some of you may want a more detailed description of your Netscape browser. Netscape has included access to a detailed set of descriptions and instructions on its homepage. To access the Netscape *Navigator Handbook*, select *Help* from the menu bar and choose *Handbook* from the menu list. This will connect you to Netscape's online handbook. Because this information is online and not held within your browser, you need an active Internet connection to use it. You can access this same information from the following URL:

http://home.netscape.com/eng/mozilla/3.0/handbook/

For information on how to get the most out of *Internet Explorer* go to the following URL:

http://www.clubie.com

The site offers information on *Explorer* features and updates, Frequently Asked Questions (FAQs), and Tips and Tricks.

Setting Options

You have several ways to customize the appearance and behavior of your browser. These customizing features are known as *Preferences* or *Options*. Descriptions for some of the *Preferences/Options* follow, as well as the reasons you might want to change them. After you investigate *Preferences/Options*, you'll be able to explore the other custom features on your own.

Navigator

Navigator lists common functions under the *Edit/Preferences* menu on the menu bar at the top of the browser window. Select *Edit* and a pop-up window will appear (Figure 3.1). Once you've selected *Preferences*, you'll notice that the preferences are broken down into categories according to function. The different categories are listed in the left pane of the window (Figure 3.2). Each category has a plus sign (+) next to it; clicking the plus sign will expand or collapse the submenu for that category. Notice that there are check marks by some of the options. Look at *Advanced/Auto Load Images*, for example. When there is a check mark,

Figure 3.1. In *Navigator,* access *Preferences* from the *Edit* menu.

29

Figure 3.2. From *Navigator's Preferences* menu, you can select options to customize your browser.

images will be loaded automatically. If you select this option again, the check mark disappears and subsequently pages will load the text without the time-consuming images. Give it a try. Additional preferences can be accessed from the other *Preferences* sub-menus.

Explorer

Internet Explorer lists common functions under the *View/Internet Options* menu (Figure 3.3). Select *Internet Options* from the *View* menu and a pop-up window will appear (Figure 3.4). You'll notice that the options are broken down into tabbed pages. Clicking on a tab will take you to the page for that category of options. Although each tabbed page is different from the next, there are instructions to guide you through the steps. For example, click on the *Advanced* tab and scroll down to *Show Pictures*. When

Figure 3.3. In *Explorer*, access *Internet Options* from the *View* menu.

Figure 3.4. In *Explorer,* you can customize your browser from the *Internet Options* menu.

there is a check mark, images will be loaded automatically. Without a check mark, pages will load the text without the time-consuming images. Additional options can be accessed from the other tabs.

Now that you know where to go to modify the setup for your browser, we'll describe some of the features you may want to modify. You will probably want to look at each preference even if you choose not to modify it. Also, keep in mind that some of these changes are not relevant to your setup; others require specific information in order for your browser to work with your ISP. You can always check the online *Navigator Handbook* for help.

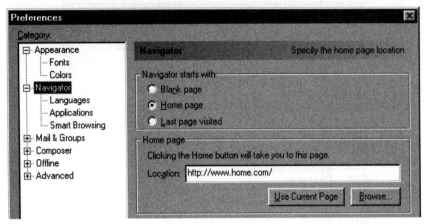

Figure 3.5. Use the *Edit/Preferences* menu in *Navigator* to designate a homepage.

Homepage

You might want to modify the location of your homepage. A homepage is like "home" in a game of hopscotch. It is the place you begin hopping from square to square. If you're working with a browser that hasn't been customized before, the company that made the browser probably chose the homepage. If you're working on one of your school's computers, then the homepage may already be set to the school's page. If you're permitted to change the homepage, then decide what you want to designate as your homepage. By now you've probably found something on the Web that you are willing to call home. When *your* homepage is properly set, every time you start your browser or select *Home* from the toolbar, you'll end up at this place.

Navigator

Open the *Edit/Preferences* menu and choose *Navigator*. To the right of the window you will see a dialog box within the *Home page* control panel (Figure 3.5) that allows you to set your homepage. Type in the URL of your new homepage.

Explorer

Open the *View/Internet Options* menu. Choose the *General* tab, where you will find a place to type in the address of your Home URL (Figure 3.6).

Figure 3.6 Use the *View/Internet Options* menu in *Explorer* to designate a home page.

Linkage

You have probably noticed that hyperlinks are normally blue (unless someone has changed the default color). Once you've accessed the page that the hyperlink represents, it changes to purple. Think of this as the bread crumb principle. The purple links remind you that you've already been down a particular path (link) and that you might want to select a different path. Eventually, however, the hyperlink will change back to its default color. But you can designate the elapsed time before a hyperlink changes back to the default color. You can also choose the default color. Generally, the more time you spend on the Internet, the more quickly (within 24 hours, for example) your links should revert to default. If you travel frequently and find that your hyperlinks are always purple, then your expiration limit may be set too long.

Figure 3.7. In *Navigator,* from the *Edit/Preferences* menu, select the *Navigator* category to access the *History* dialog box. Set the length of time for hyperlinks to expire.

Navigator

From the *Edit/Preferences* menu, open the *Preferences* window and select the *Navigator* category. At the bottom of the window, you will see a *History* dialog box that allows you to set the length of time in days for hyperlinks to expire (Figure 3.7).

Explorer

Open the *View/Internet Options* menu and choose the *General* tab (Figure 3.6). At the bottom of the window, you will see a *History* dialog box that allows you to select the length of time in days for hyperlinks to expire.

Font Style, Size, and Color

If you spend a great deal of time on the computer, then you realize the importance of adjusting your monitor, desk, and keyboard to minimize potential eye strain and muscle fatigue. Selecting a font of appropriate color, style, and size should help alleviate the hazard.

Navigator

To change the default style and size of the font, select the *Edit/Preferences* menu. Select the *Appearance/Font* category from this window. You may modify the default settings for both the font size and style used by your browser.

To view other possible font settings, select the appropriate *Font* pull-down menu (Figure 3.8). You should work primarily with the variable width font setting because it is used for the normal text on your browser. (Fixed width fonts are generally used when a page designer is illustrating computer code or text requiring uniform spacing.) In the *Font* pull-down menus you can select from numerous font styles and sizes. When you click the OK button, those font settings will be selected as the default for your browser. If you like your selection, click the OK button at the bottom of the *Fonts* window.

To change the default colors, select the *Edit/Preferences* menu.

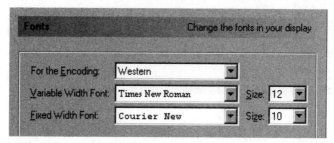

Figure 3.8. In *Navigator,* use the *Fonts* pull-down menus to select font styles and sizes.

Figure 3.9. In *Navigator,* to change the color setting click on the appropriate color button. Then click on a color in the color choices that are displayed.

Select the *Appearance/Colors* category from this window. You may modify the default color settings used by your browser for the hyperlinks (*Unvisited Links* and *Visited Links*) and regular text containing no hyperlinks (*Text*) (Figure 3.9).

To change the color setting, select the appropriate color button. A small window will appear displaying numerous color choices. Click on a color. If you like your choice, click the OK button in the *Colors* window.

Experiment with the *Colors* window. Try to modify both the text and background colors. Remember not to go overboard with your power; you still need to be able to read the words on the page. Some font colors or sizes may be difficult to read and may cause eye strain.

Explorer

Internet Explorer allows you to change font settings by opening the *View/ Internet Options* menu. Choose the *General* tab and then click on the *Fonts* button. Once there, you can change fonts depending on what is loaded into your computer (Figure 3.10). Some web sites offer versions

Figure 3.10. To change the font selection in *Explorer,* open the *View/Internet Options* menu, choose the *General* tab, and then click on the *Fonts* button.

of their site in different languages. If you need to change the *language,* follow the same process as you would to change *fonts* but this time click on the *Language* button to view and change what *languages* you may have loaded onto your computer. By clicking on the *Colors* button you may modify the default color settings for the hyperlinks and regular text. In the *Colors* box (Figure 3.11), select the appropriate color button. A small

Figure 3.11. To change the color selection in *Explorer,* open the *View/Internet Options* menu, choose the *General* tab, and then click on the *Colors* button.

Figure 3.12. Click on a color and then click the OK button.

window will appear displaying color choices; click on a color and then click the OK button (Figure 3.12).

Although we have not discussed all of the options, you probably have enough information to understand how to use them. Experiment with the settings on your own. You can always check the online *Navigator Handbook* . If you are using *Explorer* and need more help, go to the *Help* menu and select *Contents and Index*. The pop-up window contains a list of topics with more information on each.

Section 3.2
Wish you were here—Communicating

Navigator and most other browsers allow you to communicate through e-mail, newsgroups, and online interest groups. E-mail links are built into many Web pages and enable you to send correspondence directly to other people through the Internet.

E-mail
E-mail is the electronic exchange of mail among people. This exchange is from one person to one (or more) specified people. Like Web browsers and Web servers, e-mail operates according to a Client-Server model. Your client software asks a server computer for mail addressed to you.

Your mail server is operated and maintained by the administrator of your campus or ISP. Although your Web server speaks a computer protocol called HyperText Transport Protocol (HTTP), your mail server speaks a computer protocol called Simple Mail Transport Protocol (SMTP).

Think of the server as your mailbox. The mailbox is where mail addressed to you is stored until you pick it up. You use your mail client to retrieve your mail from your mailbox.

Gaining access to an e-mail server is easy. If you are at a campus that has provided you with Internet access, you should be able to apply for an e-mail account through your campus computer administrator. Otherwise, you can apply for an e-mail account through an ISP. If you use an ISP to access the Internet, you probably have e-mail capabilities. In order to properly configure your browser for sending e-mail, you need to know (1) your e-mail address and (2) the name of your mail server.

Before configuring the browser for e-mail, let's look at the form of an e-mail address: NAME@HOST.DOMAIN. It is not necessary to have a full name for the NAME part of the address; in fact, some addresses use only numbers.

The @ symbol in e-mail addresses is known simply as the "at" symbol. Around the world, it is known by more colorful names. For example, in Italy and in France it is known as "chiocciolina" and "petit escargot" (little snail); in the Netherlands it's api (short for apestaart, monkey's tail); in Norway it's "kariel-bolle" (a twisted cinnamon bun); in Denmark it's "snabel A" (an A with a trunk); in Germany it's "Klammeraffe" (spider monkey); and in Finland it's called "miau" (for another animal with a tail).

Here is a typical e-mail address.

ethiroux@worldnet.att.net

The three basic components of an e-mail address include

user name	ethiroux
host server	worldnet.att
domain	net

Send a note if you have any comments about this manual.

Your *User Name* is also the NAME associated with your e-mail address. The @ symbol always follows the NAME and then the name of the server computer (HOST). The domain in the e-mail format, just like the domain of the URL format, is used to indicate the affiliation of the user. Notice that there are no spaces anywhere in an e-mail address. Sometimes dashes, periods, or underscores are used as separators in e-mail addresses. Also, e-mail addresses are not case sensitive, so you can capitalize letters or not at your discretion.

Your campus computer administrator or your ISP will provide you with an e-mail address. This is the address you'll give to your friends. It will also be posted with any correspondence you send on the Internet.

Communicator

Configuring *Communicator*, part of your Netscape package along with *Navigator*, to send and receive e-mail only takes two steps:

First: Netscape *Communicator* includes an e-mail and newsgroup reading program called Netscape *Messenger*. To set your personal information, select the *Edit/Preferences* menu and open the *Mail and Newsgroups* window. Select the *Identity* category and you will see the text entry boxes where you can enter your information (Figure 3.13).

Figure 3.13. Configure Netscape *Communicator* to *send* e-mail by entering your personal information in the *Identity* screen. The *Signature* feature can be used to place standard information (such as your address and phone number) at the bottom of your messages.

Figure 3.14. Configure *Communicator* to *receive* e-mail by entering server information on the *Mail Server* screen.

Second: To set your e-mail information, select the *Edit/Preferences* menu and open the *Mail and Newsgroups* window. Select the *Servers* category and you will see the text entry boxes (Figure 3.14). After you've entered the correct information, restart the browser program. Now you should have the ability to send and receive e-mail. Think about it! You'll save on postage and long-distance phone bills.

Now let's send some e-mail. Select the *Communicator* option from the menu bar and choose *Messenger*. A new window will open (Figure 3.15).

Notice that this window is similar to a Web browser. (It is also similar to the news reader that we will discuss later.) To view your mail, select the *Get Msg* button. If you have mail, then it will appear in the top frame of the window. All incoming mail arrives in the *Inbox*. When you select the *Inbox* in the pull-down menu, its contents will appear in the top frame of the window. When you select a specific mail item in the top frame, you will see the contents displayed at the bottom of the window. To test the setup, send yourself an e-mail message. Next, write your congressperson. You can find his/her address in the box on page 42.

Figure 3.15. To send and receive e-mail, select the *Communicator* option from the menu bar and choose *Messenger*. The window that opens is similar to a Web browser.

Explorer

Choose the *View/Internet Options* menu, click on the *Programs* tab and then choose the *Mail* menu. From there you are allowed to select whatever "e-mail programs" you have loaded onto your computer. You fill out your exact e-mail information within your e-mail program, not within Explorer.

Most e-mail systems use a single machine to handle both incoming and outgoing mail. However, some systems use a different machine for incoming and outgoing mail. In Figure 3.14, note that two different text entry boxes are provided for the mail server. If your system uses just one machine, enter the mail server twice. The person who sets up your account should be able to give you all the information you need. If they are less than helpful, then it is generally safe to assume that the address for both your incoming and outgoing mail server is MAIL.HOST.DOMAIN.

Now that you've got the basics down, here are three sites you'll find useful.

A Beginner's Guide to Effective Email
http://www.webfoot.com/advice/email.top.html

The Electronic Activist
http://www.ifas.org/activist/index.html

Congressional E-mail Directory
http://www.webslingerz.com/jhoffman/congress-email.html

Newsgroups

Many browsers enable users to exchange ideas by using newsgroups. A newsgroup is a group of people who participate in a specialized discussion on the Internet. These groups are open forums in which all are welcomed to contribute. Newsgroup postings are sent to a common place for all to read and reply. Some are moderated by one or more people who post items for discussion and referee any electronic brawls that may ensue. However, not all newsgroups are rife with disagreement. Many offer excellent opportunities for polite conversation with courteous people. All newsgroups provide a place where people can bring new ideas and perspectives to the screen. If e-mail is like the postal service, though, newsgroups are like coffee houses on open microphone night.

What is the purpose of the newsgroups if people just contribute ideas and comments on a particular subject? Newsgroups are places where you can ask questions, get ideas, and learn about specific topics. Select a group that has an interest common to yours or a topic that you are trying to learn about. You'll find that there are many newsgroups that focus on English Literature and Composition and English Literature and Composition-related areas.

The names of newsgroups usually describe their discussion topic. There are several major newsgroup categories. The ones you'll probably use most are the ALT or REC groups. ALT stands for alternative topics, which typically encompass serious-minded or controversial social, economic, political, or religious ideas. REC sontains topics considered recreational and creative. We've included a list of relevant newsgroups in Appendix I. You'll find some of them interesting and helpful as a supplement to your studies in English Literature and Composition.

Here is a typical newsgroup URL. Newsgroup names are divided into several descriptive words separated by a period and organized according to a hierarchy. Note that newsgroup URLs don't use the double slash (//).

news:rec.arts.poems

Here are the main components:

protocol	news:
top category	rec
sub category	art
sub category	poems

To configure your browser to connect to a newsgroup, you will need the name of the server computer that handles newsgroups. (Get this from the same people who gave you your mail-server address.) You'll perform almost the same procedure you used to set up your e-mail service.

Communicator

To set your newsgroup information, select the *Edit/Preferences* menu and open the *Mail & Groups* window. Select the *Groups Server* tab and you will see the text entry boxes (Figure 3.16). Once you enter the correct information and restart the browser program, you should be able to view newsgroups. You may find that you can't access some newsgroups. Check to make sure your ISP subscribes to these groups. If not, your ISP will usually do so if you make a request.

You should now be ready for an adventure. When you use *Navigator* to read or post articles to newsgroups, you won't be using the same window that you used for browsing the Web. For newsgroups, you'll use what is typically called a *news reader*. To start your news reader, select the *Communicator* option from the menu bar and choose *Messenger* or *Collabra*, depending on your version of *Communicator*. A new window will open (Figure 3.17).

Note how this window resembles the Web browser, as well as how it differs. To view a larger list of newsgroups you can select *File/Sub-*

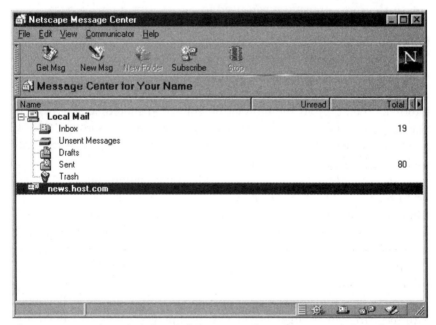

Figure 3.16. Enter server information in *Communicator's Groups Server* window to configure your browser to read newsgroups.

Figure 3.17. *Navigator* includes a built-in news reader. Its feature are similar to both the mail client and the Web browser.

scribe to Discussion Groups from the menu bar. A new window will open with tabs to view *All Groups, Search* newsgroups, and view *New* newsgroups that may have been added since you last logged on (Figure 3.18). Select *All Groups.* A large list of newsgroups will appear on the left. You can subscribe to a specific one by selecting it and then pressing the *Subscribe* button on the right; then click OK. When you are done, close this window and return to the *Messenger* or *Collabra* window. In *Collabra*, you'll immediately see the newsgroups to which you subscribed, and you will be able to read each newsgroup or article by clicking on it. In *Messenger*, you'll have to select your news server from the pull-down menu (the same pull-down where you selected your Inbox). When you select a newsgroup, the individual articles will appear in the top frame of the window. Finally, when you select a specific article, you'll see the contents displayed at the bottom of the news reader window. Now, take some time and explore.

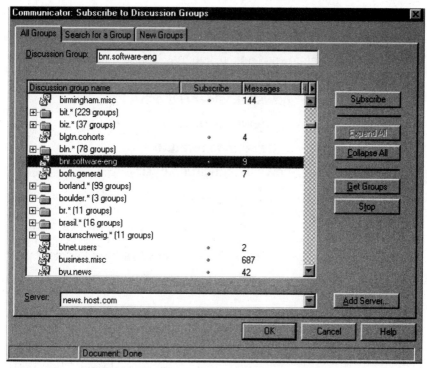

Figure 3.18. Subscribe to a specific newsgroup by selecting it and then pressing the *Subscribe* button; then click OK.

Explorer

Choose the *View/Internet Options* menu. Click on the *Programs* tab and then choose the *News* menu. From there you are allowed to choose whatever "news programs" you have loaded onto your computer. You fill out your *News* information within your *News* program, not within *Explorer*.

News servers use a protocol called *NetNews Transfer Protocol*, or *NNTP*. You might need to ask around to find out the address for your news server. If you can't find someone to help, you can probably assume that the address for your news server is NEWS.HOST.DOMAIN.

The only way to really understand what newsgroups are like is to try them. Here are a several newsgroups that will get you started. Connect to one of interest and read some of the postings. For your first time, you should just read the postings and follow some of the conversations. (This is called lurking.) Connections or threads develop between postings as people add comments to earlier postings. As you become familiar with the topic of discussion, you might post a comment yourself. Before you jump in, you may want to read the section titled "Language for the Road" in this chapter.

news:bit.listserv.edtech

news:rec.org.sca

news:tnn.literature

news:uk.education.misc

Two useful tools for newsgroups are *DejaNews* and *Reference.COM*. *DejaNews* (**http://www.dejanews.com/**) allows you to search for topics in newsgroups. *Reference.COM* (**http://www.reference.com/**) notifies you by e-mail if topics specified by you are discussed. Take a look at both of these!

Chat

This is yet another avenue for communication. It is probably the one you'll choose if you like to talk. Unlike e-mail and newsgroups, which require you to wait for a response, chat rooms are real-time. This means that you are conversing and observing conversations as they happen. As with newsgroups, it is best to observe the interactions of several chat rooms and read the new user information before you jump in. Some rooms can be excessive and vulgar, but many are frequented by polite people with a genuine desire for conversation. Just like newsgroups, chat rooms are organized by topic and you can usually anticipate the discussion by the name of the group. Unlike newsgroups, there are few academic-specific chat rooms; therefore, you'll probably find that they are a great place for general conversation.

Just to get you started, here are a few Web-based chat groups. Read the instructions and ask for help if you need it.

WebChat Broadcasting System
http://webchat5.wbs.net/

Jammin's ChatPlanet Chat Room!
http://www.jammin.com/livechat.html

Matt's PaleoChat Room
http://www.pitt.edu/~mattf/PaleoChat.html

Unlike e-mail and newsgroups, you will be frequently asked to login or register before beginning to chat. Often you'll even be given a password. Always, read the rules for participating and ask for help if you don't understand something. The participants are generally very helpful. The other characteristic of chat rooms is that typically you will use a "handle" or pseudonym when you post a message.

Language for the Road

A few words of caution. Unlike normal conversations between people, electronic exchanges don't convey vocal inflections, facial expression, and body language. (These things aren't easily digitized and transmitted across a copper wire. To be sure, there are such things as Internet telephones and video conferencing, but for most of us they are not affordable and practical.) You will need to practice the way you communicate electronically and be patient when someone misinterprets something you've "said." For example, suppose you tell a joke. Because the reader only gets the text, she may think that you are serious and take offense. Computer people learned about this problem a long time ago and an innovative solution has been developed. The solution is a collection of "smileys."

Here are some smileys; tilt your head to the left to interpret them:

:-)	smile	:-x	my lips are sealed
;-)	wink	:-o	oh!
:- (	sad	:-I	indifferent
:-[	very sad	:-*	kiss

Because you will eventually get tired of typing all of the things you want to say, several acronyms are in common use. Here are a few:

BTW	By The Way
IMHO	In My Humble Opinion
FYI	For Your Information
FWIW	For What It's Worth
TIA	Thanks in Advance
ADN	Any Day Now
B4N	Bye For Now

Now for a couple of terms. Like any other culture, the Internet community has borrowed some common words to describe special situations. Here are two that you'll see:

Flame This refers to the act of yelling, insulting, or degrading a person or his or her character. You can expect to get flamed if you don't follow certain basic rules of netiquette (etiquette of the Net).
Spam This refers to the act of posting a comment, message, or advertisement to multiple newsgroups when the note doesn't really pertain to the newsgroup topic. It is the Internet equivalent of sending junk mail.

Here are a couple of Web resources that you will want to read when you begin communicating online. They are very helpful and entertaining. Enjoy!

E-Mail Etiquette
http://www.iwillfollow.com/email.htm

Electronic Frontier Foundation's Unofficial Smiley Dictionary
http://www.eff.org/papers/eegtti/eeg_286.html

Section 3.3
The fun is in the going—Extending

In early Web history, travel was pretty basic. The browser was a piece of software that acted as a totally self-contained vehicle. When you hooked it up, it contained everything you needed to cruise the Net. This has changed. As the Web grows larger, people develop new formats of information they wish to include on the Web. These new formats allow for a richer expression. Things like digital video, audio, animations, interactive games, and 3D worlds are currently very common on the Internet. As people demand more functionality from the Internet, new formats will become available. To cope with this continuing change, Netscape and *Explorer* developed a way to add functionality without overloading the basic browser design.

Helpers and Plug-ins

Early Web pages included only text and images. They were much like brochures with the ability to hyperlink to other pages. The images that were included in Web pages were in a GIF format. However, to accommodate new image formats like JPEG, browsers turned to helper applications. If a page designer included a JPEG image, then an external helper application program displayed the image for viewing outside of the browser. Rather than having to rely on external programs, plug-in programs were developed to add the same features within the browser itself. For example, if you want to listen to music across the Internet from your browser, then you could install a plug-in that allows the browser to understand the audio format.

Netscape and *Explorer* have developed many plug-ins, and they are still the place to turn when you want one. An important thing, though: adding plug-ins to your browser will increase your memory (RAM) requirements. If you add too many plug-ins, your browser might stop working. Only install the plug-ins that you're going to use regularly.

These addresses will take you to the place where you can download the plug-ins to your computer. The developers also provide a very good description of how to install and use the plug-ins.

RealAudio by Progressive Networks
http://www.real.com/products/player/index.html

Java and JavaScript

Grab a cup of coffee for this one. Helper application programs (helpers) and plug-ins weren't enough to satisfy Web developers. Web developers wanted even more—*more* flexibility, *more* interactivity, and *more* control. *Java* and *JavaScript* were developed to provide the more that developers wanted. But to understand what Java and JavaScript are, you need to understand what Web pages *were not*. Web page designers didn't claim to *program* Web pages; rather, they said that they *wrote, designed,* or *created* Web pages. You may wonder what the difference is. Programming is the process of developing a set of instructions that perform a specific function. Writing, designing, and creating are activities that communicate ideas. When executed, programs actively do things, whereas Web pages communicate ideas (by bringing together different media).

One type of media, interactive programs, did not exist in Web pages until the programming languages *Java* and *JavaScript* were made available. Now, besides communicating ideas, Web pages can also interactively do things as well. They add functionality to Web pages just as helpers and plug-ins do, but they provide much greater flexibility. The fundamental difference between the two languages is that *JavaScript* is usually integrated with the Web page and runs on the client side, whereas *Java* is usually integrated on the server side. The results are probably best understood by examining a few *Java* and *JavaScript* programs for yourself. If you are using Netscape *Navigator 2.0* or greater (or Microsoft *Internet*

Explorer 3.0 or greater), then you have the ability to view and interact with these programs, although the 4.0 versions do a much better job at handling all flavors of Javascript. But a word of caution here, not all Javascript is created equal. Do not be surprised if a web page appears and functions correctly in *Navigator* and then fails to appear or work correctly while being viewed in *Explorer*, or vice versa. This can happen for a variety of reasons but it most often occurs when Javascripting is involved. Most quality sites will take the differences of the two browsers into account but even then some strange things can and do happen.

The first three URLs will connect you to some really interesting examples of *Java*.

The Impressionist
   http://reality.sgi.com/paul_asd/impression/

Crossword Puzzle
   http://home.netscape.com/comprod/products/navigator/version_2.0/
   java_applets/Crossword

Java Applets
   http://www.javasoft.com:80/applets/

This last URL will connect you to a rather large collection of both *Java* and *JavaScript* examples.

Gamelan
   http://www.developer.com

Depending on your system, these examples may take a while to load, so be patient.

There are two other developments in web creation that should also be mentioned: Cascading style sheets and dynamic HTML. Cascading style sheets are a major improvement in Web development because they allow Web designers to control the style and layout of multiple Web pages all at once. Cascading style sheets work like templates. Web developers define a style for an HTML element and then apply it to as many Web pages as they need. Utilizing CSS, when you want to make a change, you change the style, and that element is updated automatically wherever it appears within the site, whereas before CSS each element would have to be individually updated. *Navigator 4.0* and *Explorer 4.0* both support cascading style sheets.

Dynamic HTML is a combination of HTML, scripting (mostly Javascripting), and CSS that helps create robust, interactive Web pages without increasing the download times for these pages to be viewed. The standards for dynamic HTML are still being hammered out and *Navigator* and *Explorer* are handling it in different ways, so expect differences.

http://www.stars.com/Authoring/Style/Sheets/

http://www.htmlhelp.com/reference/css/

If you want to see Dynamic HTML in action go to Macromedia's Dynamic HTML Zone at **http://www.dhtmlzone.com/alt.html.** Remember that you must have a 4.0 version of *Navigator* or *Explorer* to view much of this.

Activity:
A Talkabout Tour

Learning doesn't stop when you leave the classroom or laboratory. The people around you, textbooks, libraries, and the Internet are all important resources that broaden your education. In particular, the Web, newsgroups, chat rooms, and e-mail can all help you become well-rounded and well-connected.

E-mail

Because you have a wealth of information at your fingertips, take the time to get some e-mail addresses from your instructor or other students. Most good e-mail software will provide you with a mechanism to store these addresses for easy retrieval. Begin exchanging e-mail with some of these people and you'll find that there is plenty of help available when you need it.

Newsgroups

Make it a practice to browse newsgroups. Plenty are of general interest; you should also make a habit of checking into a newsgroup that focuses on important topics discussed in class. By visiting many different newsgroups, you'll always have the latest scoop in a variety of subjects.

Chat

Chat rooms may or may not enhance your education. However, you might be able to find a chat room that is relatively empty. If so, arrange a fixed weekly time when you and your classmates can get together to work out problems or discuss material covered that week. A better option is to meet in person, but if this is impossible, chat rooms can provide an alternative.

Web Page

If you are using an ISP for Internet access, then you probably have access to posting information on your homepage. Consider using it as a way to bring other students together for discussion. Check with your instructor and you may find that he or she is willing to help you with this activity.

Chapter 4
A Unique Online Study Resource
The Companion Website™

As a student you are no doubt familiar with the various supplements produced in conjunction with your textbooks. From videotapes to workbooks, these tools are designed to reinforce the core concepts presented by textbook authors. In addition to traditional print study guides, Prentice Hall now offers online study guides called Companion Websites. To date, over 1,000,000 students like you have visited Prentice Hall's text-specific Companion Websites.

Prentice Hall Companion Websites allow you to:

- identify key topics in your course.
- take interactive quizzes.
- receive immediate feedback on your answers.
- send your results to instructors via e-mail.
- search the Internet using links that have been selected by field experts.

Companion Websites are easy to use. Their standardized design leads you carefully from one activity to the next, chapter by chapter. Online study guides not only give you a better understanding of the core concepts presented in your textbooks, but they also focus your attention on the most important material in every chapter. Most of all, Companion Websites help you use your study time more effectively.

Section 4.1
Locating Companion Websites

Not sure if your book has a Companion Website? Visiting the Prentice Hall Companion Website Gallery is the simplest way to find out. Go to the

Prentice Hall website at **http://www.prenhall.com** and click on *Companion Website Gallery* in the upper right-hand corner of the screen. Then, in the empty box on the black navigation bar, enter the last name of your textbook's author. To generate a list of websites that meet your criteria, click on the *Search* button. For example, a search for "Faragher" would yield the screen shown in Figure 4.1.

Figure 4.1. Entering an author's name and clicking on the *Search* button will generate a list of Websites that meet your criteria.

Select the appropriate book by looking at the covers, hyperlinked titles, and brief descriptions.

Notice that some sites are labeled "demo." As such sites are currently under development, you can access only one or two chapters of sample content. Check back frequently since Prentice Hall is constantly adding new titles to the Companion Website Gallery.

Another way to see whether a particular book has a Companion Website is to type the following URL into your Location Toolbar: **http://www.prenhall.com/(lead author)**. The text in parenthesis should be replaced with the name of the lead author of your Prentice Hall textbook. For example, the address for *Arts and Culture* by Janetta Rebold Benton and Robert DiYanni is **http://www.prenhall.com/benton**.

Section 4.2
Getting Started

On the first page of every Humanities and Social Sciences Companion Website you will find two frames (Figure 4.2):

Left frame: Navigation Bar

- Syllabus Manager™
- Carol Carter's Student Success Web Supersite
- Your Profile
- Help

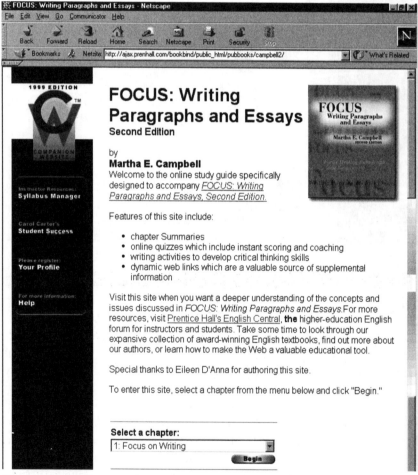

Figure 4.2. The first page of every Companion Website is divided into two frames: the navigation bar and the content window.

Right frame: Content Window

- Link to Web Catalog
- Website Features
- Chapter Menu
- Begin Button

This section will walk you through each of these components.

Navigation Bar

Syllabus Manager

Every Companion Website integrates Syllabus Manager, an online syllabus creation and management utility. After an instructor has created a syllabus using Syllabus Manager, students may enter the syllabus for their course section from any point in the Companion Website. To see whether your instructor has created an online syllabus for your course, click on the *Syllabus Manager* or *Syllabus* button. In the Student Login Window (Figure 4.3), you have the option of searching by *Instructor's Last Name, Instructor's E-Mail Address,* or *School Name.*

After choosing the button next to your instructor's name, click on the *Search Now* button at the bottom of the screen.

Note that your instructor can create different syllabi for each section he or she teaches; be sure to check the section column (Figure 4.4) before you click on *Open Syllabus.* If your instructor has password-protected the syllabus, you will need to enter the correct password in

Syllabus Manager™   A Course Building Tool for Online Course Companion™

Student Login

If your instructor has prepared a syllabus online, you may "turn it on" so that it's viewable as a part of this Online Course Companion. Begin by searching for your instructor's syllabus:

Search By : ⊙ Instructor's Last Name
             ○ Instructor's E-Mail Address
             ○ School Name

Moore   (**Search Now**)

Figure 4.3. Use the Student Login Window to see whether your instructor has created an online syllabus for your course.

Search Result

Last, First Name	School Name
○ MCPHAUL-MOORE, ELIZABETH	PIEDMONT COMMUNITY COLLEGE
○ Moore, Chris	Citrus College
○ Moore, Gene	Lake Region High School
◉ Moore, Gina	Pearson University
○ moore, Jason	cal st fullerton
○ Moore, John	Tidewater Community College

Figure 4.4. When the search engine generates a list of several syllabi, make sure you select the syllabus for your section.

the Logon screen (Figure 4.5) before you can continue. Lost passwords can be requested by using the form at the bottom of the screen.

After you gain access to the correct syllabus, course summary information appears in the right frame and a calendar appears in the left frame

Syllabi for Professor Moore

Course Name	Section	Security
◉ History	101	Password Not Required

Student Password: [＿＿＿＿＿＿＿＿] (**Open Syllabus**)

Lost Password

If you don't know the password, you can send e-mail to professor for access to a particular syllabus. Please select the syllabus from above and fill out your email address and a short note if needed.

Your Full Name : [＿＿＿＿＿＿＿＿＿＿＿]

Your E-Mail Address : [＿＿＿＿＿＿＿＿＿＿＿]

Note : [＿＿＿＿＿＿＿＿＿＿＿]

Help

Figure 4.5. Fill out the login screen to enter your syllabus.

Figure 4.6. Click on a blue assignment due date on the calendar in the left frame to view the homework for that particular class.

of the Companion Website (Figure 4.6). Class dates are highlighted in white, and assignment due dates appear in blue. Clicking on a blue date reveals the assignment for that particular day. To save time, the Companion Website activities for each assignment are linked directly from the syllabus to actual content modules.

Use the following directions to print your syllabus:

- Select the syllabus frame by clicking anywhere on the white background of the syllabus.
- Select *File* from top menu bar and then select *Print Frame* ...
- Make proper printer settings and click *OK*.

Carol Carter's Student Success Web Supersite

Geared towards high school graduates, college students, returning students, and career changers, this resource site is designed to help students select the appropriate path to meet their educational needs. Features include:

- exploration of different majors.
- answers to study skill questions.
- advice from career counselors.
- brief biographies designed to inspire lifelong learners.
- Web links to interesting sites related to student success.

Your Profile

As mentioned in the overview, Companion Websites not only allow you to take interactive quizzes, but they also give you the opportunity to send your results to an instructor via e-mail. The *Profile* feature lets you standardize the submission of your quiz results. By (carefully) entering your personal information in Figure 4.7, you can avoid retyping it every time you need to submit homework. Once saved, the information will appear automatically whenever it's required. Remember that you MUST click on the *E-mail Results* button in the *Results Reporter* each time you want to send data to your instructor.

You may return to this screen to modify your profile at any time by clicking the *Profile* button located on the navigation bar throughout the site.

Personal Information

	First	Last
My Name:		
E-mail:		

Instructor Information

	Name	E-Mail
Instructor:		
TA:		
Other:		

Figure 4.7. This form gives you the opportunity to send your results to an instructor via e-mail. By carefully entering your personal information, you can avoid retyping it every time you need to submit homework.

Send my quiz results to:

☐	Myself:	As plain text ▾
☐	Instructor:	As plain text ▾
☐	TA:	As plain text ▾
☐	Other:	As plain text ▾

Figure 4.8. By filling out this form you not only select the recipients of your quiz results, but you also select the format of your messages.

After you enter your personal data, remember to check the all of the appropriate boxes under "Send my quiz results to" (Figure 4.8). If you and your recipients prefer to receive your results in the body of an e-mail message, select either "as plain text" or "as HTML" (for *Navigator* or *Internet Explorer* e-mail). On the other hand, if you and your recipients prefer to receive your results as an attachment, select either "as text attachment" or "as HTML attachment" (for *Navigator* or *Internet Explorer* e-mail). Please note that you should always e-mail yourself a copy of your results because Prentice Hall will not save a backup copy.

Due to the volume of submissions, Companion Website e-mail is batched and sent out at thirty minute intervals. Depending on when you send your results to our server for distribution, it may take up to thirty minutes for your results to arrive in your professor's inbox. Keep this in mind when submitting homework assignments.

In the *Profile* area you can also subscribe to the site mailing list by entering your name and e-mail address. Companion Website mailing lists alert users of site updates, i-Chat events, and other items directly related to the textbook or website. Prentice Hall does not use mailing lists for marketing or "spam" e-mail purposes.

Help

This brief overview of Companion Website technology addresses questions that other users have had in the past. Topics are organized by module type in the left-hand navigation bar. To learn more about a particular feature, simply click on its name.

Content Window

In addition to a list of website features, the content window on the first page of every Companion Website contains a link to the Web Catalog.

Select a chapter:

1: Worlds Apart ▼

Begin

Figure 4.9. To enter a Companion Website, select a chapter from the pull-down menu at the bottom of the screen and click *Begin*.

Visit the Web Catalog to read a summary of the textbook and view a complete table of contents. To enter the site, (1) select a chapter from the pull-down menu at the bottom of the screen and (2) click *Begin* (Figure 4.9).

Section 4.3
Navigation

In order to move through a Companion Website effectively, you should use the navigation bar in the left frame of the browser window. The top of the navigation bar (Figure 4.10) offers controls for moving to the previous chapter, the next chapter, or to the top of the site (the index page).

Figure 4.10. The top of the navigation bar offers controls for moving to the previous chapter, the next chapter, or to the top of the site (the index page).

The middle of the navigation bar (Figure 4.11) provides links directly to the quiz, research, and communication modules discussed later in this document. Sometimes this area will also include links to individual modules that have been gathered into groups.

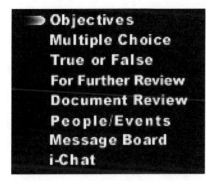

Figure 4.11. The middle of the navigation bar provides links directly to the quiz, research, and communication modules.

The bottom portion of the navigation bar (Figure 4.12) contains links to the Help files, User Profile, Feedback, Site Search, and Course Syllabus, if available.

Figure 4.12. The bottom portion of the navigation bar contains links to the help files, user profile, feedback, site search, and course syllabus.

Section 4.4
The Modules

Objectives
The opening page of every chapter defines the unit by providing a summary of the topics covered. This summary can be a list of learning goals for the chapter, a brief introduction/overview of the chapter, or a combination of the two formats.

Multiple Choice
As in traditional learning environments, *Multiple Choice* quizzes are one of the most popular methods of online testing. In fact, the majority of Prentice Hall Companion Websites include at least one *Multiple Choice*

quiz. Depending on which book you are using, this quiz module may have a name other than "Multiple Choice." Sample names range from "Review I" to "Elements."

Figure 4.13. This is an example of a *Multiple Choice* question.

Figure 4.13 is from an actual *Multiple Choice* quiz module. Each question consists of the following elements:

- the question.
- a *Hint* that will open in a new, smaller browser window.
- the possible answers.

In order to select an answer, mark the circle in front of it with your mouse. When you have completed the quiz, click on the *Submit for Grade* button at the bottom of the page to send your answers to the *Results Reporter* (see page 69).

True or False

True or False quizzes are another popular feature of Companion Websites. Depending on the book you are using, this module may have a name other than "True or False."

Figure 4.14. This is an example of a True or False question.

Figure 4.14 is an example from an actual *True or False* quiz module. Each question consists of the following elements:

- the question.
- a *Hint* that will open in a new, smaller browser window.
- the two possible answers.

In order to select an answer, mark the circle in front of it with your mouse. When you have completed the quiz, click on the *Submit for Grade* button at the bottom of the page to send your answers to the *Results Reporter* (see page 69).

Fill in the Blanks

Depending on which book you are using, this quiz module may have a name other than "Fill in the Blanks."

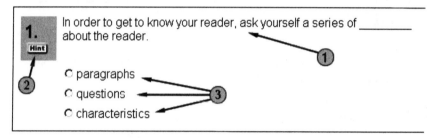

Figure 4.15. This is an example of a *Fill in the Blanks* question. Its format is the same as a traditional *Multiple Choice* question.

Figure 4.15 is from an actual *Fill in the Blanks* quiz module. Each question consists of the following elements:

- the question with a blank line.
- a *Hint* that will open in a new, smaller browser window.
- a list of possible answers that could fill in the blank line.

In order to select an answer, mark the circle in front of it with your mouse. When you have completed the quiz, click on the *Submit for Grade* button at the bottom of the page to send your answers to the *Results Reporter* (see page 69).

Essay

Depending on the book you are using, this quiz module may have a name other than Essay. Some examples include "Historical Content" and "Journal Assignment." *Essay* modules may contain a block of introductory text and/or images before the questions.

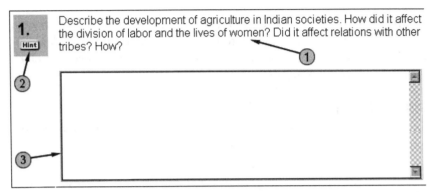

Figure 4.16. This is an example of an *Essay* question.

Figure 4.16 is from an actual *Essay* module. Each question consists of the following elements:

- a question.
- an optional *Hint* that will open in a new, smaller browser window.
- a large box, in which you type (or cut-and-paste from another application) your essay.

When you have completed the quiz, click on the *Submit for Grade* button at the bottom of the page to send your answers to the *Results Reporter* (see page 69). Essay questions have to be manually graded by your instructor, but the *Results Reporter* will tell which questions you answered and may give you some general feedback.

Pattern Match

Pattern Match is the newest addition to the Companion Website question library. Although similar in format to traditional *Fill in the Blanks* questions, *Pattern Match* eliminates the list of possible choices, forcing you to generate your own answer. Depending on what book you are using, this quiz module may have a name other than "Pattern Match."

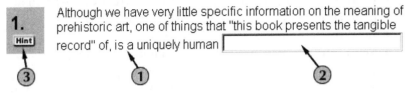

Figure 4.17. This is an example of a *Pattern Match* question.

Figure 4.17 is from a *Pattern Match* quiz module. Each question consists of the following elements:

- the question.
- a *Hint* that will open in a new, smaller browser window.
- a text entry box.

To enter an answer, click your cursor within the box and begin typing. When you have completed the quiz, click on the *Submit for Grade* button at the bottom of the page to send your answers to the *Results Reporter* (see page 69).

Matching

Matching exercises are grouped to present a series of questions in one column and a series of possible answers in another column. The questions and answers can be either text or small images. Depending on which book you are using, this quiz module may have a name other than "Matching."

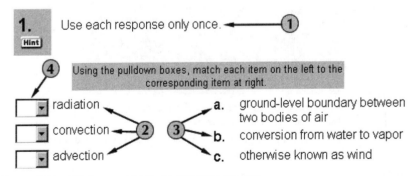

Figure 4.18. This is an example of a *Matching* question.

Figure 4.18 is from a *Matching* quiz module. To answer this type of question:

- Read the instructions. Click on the *Hint* link if you need some help. *Hints* will open in a new, smaller browser window.
- Read the term in the left column.
- Select on your response from the column on the right.
- Choose your response from the drop-down menu on the left. The letters in each menu correspond with those in the column on the right.

When you have completed the quiz, click on the *Submit for Grade* button at the bottom of the page to send your answers to the *Results Reporter* (see page 69).

Labeling

Labeling exercises consist of images with letters that correspond to specific areas. To identify the areas, you select terms from a list of below the image. Depending on which book you are using, this quiz module may have a name other than "Labeling."

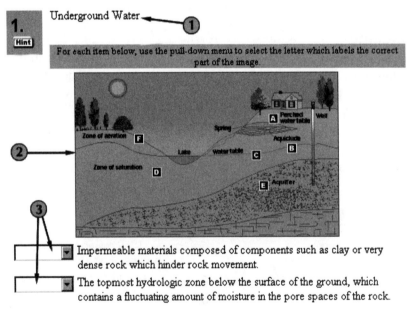

Figure 4.19. This is an example of a *Labeling* question.

Figure 4.19 is from a *Labeling* quiz module. To answer the questions:

- Read the introductory text. Click on the *Hint* link if you need some help. *Hints* will open in a new, smaller browser window.
- Examine the image.
- After reading the terms or descriptions, use the pull-down menus to select the letter that corresponds with the text to the right of the menu.

When you have completed the quiz, click on the *Submit for Grade* button at the bottom of the page to send your answers to the *Results Reporter* (see below).

Results Reporter

Once you have submitted your work through the *Submit* button, your answers are passed to the automatic grader and your grades are displayed in the *Results Reporter*. This section will explain what each part of the *Results Reporter* displays.

The first part of the *Results Reporter* summarizes how you did, beginning with the percentage of questions you answered correctly (in Figure 4.20, 70%). You are also shown graphically how many questions you answered correctly and/or incorrectly, as well as the number of questions you didn't answer. Sometimes, the *Results Reporter* will include information about the amount of time you took to complete the quiz. The grading of *Essay* modules cannot be automated so the *Results Reporter* will only display a listing of how many questions you answered.

Summary: 70% Correct

70%

30%

0%

Of 10 questions, you answered:
■ 7 correct
■ 3 incorrect
□ 0 unanswered

Figure 4.20. The first part of the *Results Reporter* summarizes how you did, beginning with the percentage of questions you answered correctly. You are also shown graphically how many questions you answered correctly and/or incorrectly, as well as the number of questions you didn't answer.

The bulk of the *Results Reporter* is a question-by-question examination of your responses which looks like this:

1. Incorrect   Marriage forms are similar across social and cultural groups.
Your Answer: TRUE
The correct answer: FALSE

The correct answer is FALSE because marriage forms vary across societal and cultural groups (see p. 2).

The top line shows the question number, whether you got the answer Correct or Incorrect, and the text of the question. Next, the *Results Reporter* lists **Your answer** and **The correct answer**. Finally, depending upon the book you are using, the report may include an explanation of why your answer was correct or incorrect and where to look for additional information in your textbook.

At the bottom of the *Results Reporter* screen you can enter contact information for the people to whom you would like to send your grades (Figure 4.21). If your recipients prefer to receive your results in the

Routing Information

You may pre-set these fields, and choose other e-mail preferences by clicking the "Your Profile" button at left.

My name is:

[   ]

E-mail my results to:

	E-mail address:	Send as:
Me:	[ ]	Text
Instructor:	[ ]	Text
TA:	[ ]	Text
Other:	[ ]	Text

E-Mail Results

Figure 4.21. By filling out this form you not only select the recipients of your quiz results, but you also select the format of your messages.

body of an e-mail message, select either "as plain text" or "as HTML" (for Netscape or *Explorer* e-mail). On the other hand, if your recipients prefer to receive your results as an attachment, select either "as text attachment" or "as HTML attachment" (for *Navigator* or *Explorer* e-mail). Please note that you should always e-mail yourself a copy of your results because Prentice Hall will not save a backup copy.

As discussed earlier, the *Profile* feature lets you standardize the submission of your quiz results. By (carefully) entering your personal information in this screen, you can avoid retyping it every time you need to submit homework. Once saved, the information will appear automatically whenever it's required.

Remember that you MUST click on the *E-mail Results* button at the bottom of the *Results Reporter* each time you want to send results to an instructor.

Destinations

This module contains a list of Internet resources relevant to the work in your course. Depending on which book you are using, this module may have a name other than "Destinations." Common titles include "Web Destinations" and "Online Resources."

Each *Destinations* entry will look like this:

Prentice Hall
On Prentice Hall's Website you will find a catalog of Prentice Hall books and Companion Websites that supplement their Higher Education textbooks.

Please note that these resources generally link to sites outside of Prentice Hall. To visit a particular site, click on the underlined word or phrase (the hypertext link). This link will open a new, smaller browser window containing the information you requested. When finished with the link, return to your Companion Website by closing the smaller window.

Net Search

Net Search allows you to search the Internet based on keywords specified in each Companion Website chapter. Depending on the book you are using, this module may have a name other than "Net Search."

Use the following list to search the Internet for information related to these people and events. ①

Search Terms:
- Ferdinand and Isabella
- Paleo-Indians
- Black Death
- Protestant Reformation ②
- Ponce de León
- Bartolomeu Días
- Vasco da Gama
- St. Augustine
- Hernán Cortés
- Queen Elizabeth I

Search the Web:
Select one or more of the search terms in the list at right, then use the search buttons below to find pages on the Web which include those terms.

Search in: HotBot ▼ Search
③   ④   Reset

Figure 4.22. *Net Search* allows you to search the Internet based on keywords specified in each Companion Website chapter.

Figure 4.22 is from a *Net Search* module. To use *Net Search*:

- Read the introductory text, which may include specific instructions or other guidance on how to conduct a search for the terms listed.
- Click on one or more keywords from the list of terms. The term or terms will be added to the empty text box. You can also type in terms of your own or add Boolean operators, such as AND, NOT, OR, +, etc.
- Select a search engine from the pull-down menu.
- Click on the *Search* button to execute your search.

If your search doesn't yield the results you desire, select another one of the search engines from the pull-down menu and try again.

Message Board
Prentice Hall Message Boards use browser technology to provide students and instructors with a national forum to discuss topics related to their studies.

Configuring Your Browser for Prentice Hall Message Boards

If your system is configured correctly, when you access a Prentice Hall Message Board through a Companion Website, you will already be viewing the virtual bulletin board in your browser. If this is not the case, you are probably configured incorrectly. See the *Online Help* files for instructions on configuring your software.

Reading Messages

Upon entering the message board (Figure 4.23), you will see a list of messages in the lower portion of the screen. If there are replies to a message, they will be presented in a hierarchy that displays the reply structure. To see this hierarchy, click on the plus side on the *All* button or on the small green arrows next to the subject titles. Groups of related messages are commonly called *threads* of conversation.

Subject ▼	Sender ▼	Date ▼
No Subject	Doe, Anonymous	12/18/98 01:28 PM
▷2301-090 with prof crane	Doe, Anonymous	01/12/99 06:40 PM
pysc 2301-90 prof crane	kingsbury, lisa	01/22/99 12:15 PM
quiz	Doe, Anonymous	02/07/99 10:58 PM
Class Project	Doe, Anonymous	02/13/99 10:11 PM
No Subject	Doe, Anonymous	02/22/99 01:02 PM
▷Psyc6170-01	Guimaraes, Debora	03/01/99 02:06 PM
▷Downloads	Becker, Catherine	03/02/99 12:02 PM
▷6170	Sexton, Ginna	03/05/99 10:45 AM
6170-01	Baptista, Niosoty	03/09/99 06:27 PM

Figure 4.23. Upon entering the message board, you will see a list of messages in the lower portion of the screen.

Click on a subject title, and the message will appear in the lower window of the browser above a navigation bar (Figure 4.24). Use the buttons to read through the messages in a conversation, move to another thread, or return to the main list of postings.

From: Jacob Schwartz

Date: 04/13/99 03:15 PM

Subject: Ch. 6: memory

Message: Does anyone know the difference between Episodal Memory and Auto-Biographical memory? They sound like the same thing. Thanx. Jacob Schwartz jwschwartz@juno.com

[Reply to Message]

[◀◀ previous thread] [◀ previous message] [▲ back to threaded list] [▶ next message] [▶▶ next thread]

Figure 4.24. Messages appear in the lower window above a navigation bar.

To post a message, select the *Post New Message* button above the main index of messages (Figure 4.23). When the form opens in the lower frame (Figure 4.25), enter your name, subject title, and message in the

Post a New Message

From (First Name):

From (Last Name):

Subject:

Message:

[Done – Post Message] [Cancel]

Figure 4.25. To post a message to a message board, click on the *Post New Message* button.

appropriate fields. When you are finished, click on the *Done – Post Message* button to post your comments to the message board. You can leave this screen at any time by clicking the *Cancel* button.

To encourage discussion and debate, your reply to an existing message can be associated with an original posting. In order to do this, view the message to which you would like to respond and click on the *Reply to Message* button in the upper left-hand corner of the window (Figure 4.24). You will be presented with a window similar to the form for creating new messages, but the *Subject* field will be automatically generated (Figure 4.26). Enter your name and message in the appropriate fields. When you are finished, click on the *Done – Post Message* button to post your comments to the message board. You can leave this screen at any time by clicking the *Cancel* button.

Reply to Message

From (First Name):

From (Last Name):

Subject: Re: Ch. 6: memory

Message:

[Done -- Post Message]   [Cancel]

Figure 4.26. When replying to a message, the Subject field will be automatically generated.

i-Chat

I-Chat not only allows instructors to host private class discussions, invite guest speakers to class, and reach students easily, but it also gives you the opportunity to meet students from around the world. In order to gain full functionality of Prentice Hall chat rooms, we recommend that you use the *i-Chat* plug-in. If you choose not to do so, *i-Chat* is also accessible using Java or HTML clients (your browser will automatically select the client that provides the most features).

To enter *i-Chat*:

- Download the *i-Chat* plug-in (accessible from our tune-up page).
- Click on the *i-Chat* button on your Companion Website navigation bar.
- Enter a nickname for yourself.
- Select your chat type. We recommend the default setting.
- Click on the *Enter Chat Area* button.

Although the top region may contain some introductory text or instructions, the bottom region is the actual *i-Chat* client area (Figure 4.27). Your name and the name of the other users will appear in this area as will the text of the chat. At the bottom of the chat client area, you will find the text entry area. You can begin to participate by simply typing a message into this region and pressing *Enter*.

Once you've mastered the basics of chatting, you may want to experiment with the additional menu choices available. For help when you are in *i-chat,* use the help icon that resembles a book with a question mark.

Figure 4.27. At the bottom of the chat client area, you will find the text entry area. You can begin to participate by simply typing a message into this region and pressing *Enter.*

Advanced i-Chat *Features*

Sending Private Messages. Private messages can be sent to individual users through the client menu bar. Click on the icon of the person in silhouette. A new window asking for the recipient and the private message will be generated.

Creating a Private Room for Your Online Study Group. Private rooms can also be set up for discussions limited to only a few people. One member of the group should create the room using the *Create Private Room* option under the *Commands* sub-menu of the chat menu. Fill out the form requesting a private room. If you have a URL you would like to display in the banner, type it in the URL field; otherwise you can use a default URL such as **http://www.prenhall.com**. In order for others to join you in the room, you have to invite them by using the *linvite {username}* command.

The room will be removed when all participants have left. Private rooms can be exited by using the Navigation sub-menu of the chat menu, or by using the *lgo {exitname}* command.

Groups

Groups can have many names, but their basic premise is to gather several quiz, research, or communication modules into one area, thereby reducing clutter on the navigation bar. Figure 4.28 is an example of a group that contains several quizzes. Typical groups contain navigation icons and some instructions.

Other Modules

Because technology changes rapidly, you may encounter modules in a Companion Website that are not covered in this book. Most often the URLs for such modules will contain the words "custom.html." As Pren-

Figure 4.28. This is an example of a group of modules. Note that the icons work just like the ones in the main navigation bar.

tice Hall introduces new technologies to Companion Websites, helpful instructions will be incorporated within the modules as well as within the online *Help* pages. If you can't find an answer to your problems within these pages, please contact Prentice Hall's help support staff via e-mail:

web_tech_support@prenhall.com

To help in answering your questions quickly, please carefully describe your problem(s) and the browser you are using.

Appendix I
Internet Resources for English

A hot medium is one that extends the single sense in "high definition."
High definition is the state of being filled with data.

Here are a number of links that you should find "ve-e-ry interesting." Think of this as a starter kit for further investigation. It includes websites for using the Internet, digital library websites, and general websites for English Composition and Literature. Sites are provided for English and useful English-related sites, followed by some examples of English newsgroups.

We'd like to get faculty and student input on improving the English and English-related sites. What sites should be included in the future that students have found especially useful? Which URLs are the least informative? Please send all suggestions to **ethiroux@worldnet.att.net**.

Prentice Hall now provides active websites for many of the textbooks it publishes. These sites contain numerous links to English resources on the Internet. Simply go to the sites indicated and select the sections entitled "Web Links" or "Destinations." These Prentice Hall websites have the added advantage of providing active links to many of the resources you will find below. The Prentice Hall English URLs are:

Thiroux THE CRITICAL EDGE: THINKING AND RESEARCHING
IN A VIRTUAL SOCIETY
http://www.prenhall.com/books/hss_0137592264.html

Fulwiler/Hayakawa THE BLAIR HANDBOOK Second Edition
http://www.prenhall.com/fulwiler/

Hawisher LITERACY, TECHNOLOGY, AND SOCIETY
http://www.prenhall.com/~bookbind/pubbooks/hawisher1/

Miller NEW WAYS OF WRITING
http://www.prenhall.com/~bookbind/pubbooks/miller/

Rodriques RESEARCH PAPERS AND THE WORLD WIDE WEB
http://www.prenhall.com/~bookbind/pubbooks/rodrigues/

Several comments are in order before you begin surfing. First, don't be discouraged if your first try to link to a site produces a message like "Unable to connect to remote host." The rule of thumb is to try the same site three times in a row before proceeding to another URL. (Remember, you're still trying to communicate with the World Wide Wait.) Second, be careful typing site locations. If you mistype one character (capital letters matter), the address won't work. Third, Web sites come and go more often than print media. What is on the Internet today may be gone tomorrow. Fourth, a tilde (~) usually designates a site maintained by a person, rather than an organization or some "non-person." These are the sites most likely to disappear on the Web. Finally, we list just a few newsgroups. If you are an archaeologist (or anyone who has done some digging), there are more newsgroups than you could possibly dream of excavating. Try http://www.tile.net/tile/news/ to unearth your favorite newsgroup. Get down!

Websites for Using the Internet

Internet Starter Kit (Macmillan Computer Publishing)
http://www.mcp.com/resources/geninternet/

Web Resources
http://www.w3.org

World Wide Web FAQ
http://sunsite.unc.edu/boutell/faq/faq.txt

Learn the Net
http://www.learnthenet.com/english/index.html

Understanding and Using the Internet
http://www2.pbs.org/uti/

Newbie Training
http://www.newbie.net/CyberCourse

The Internet for Social Scientists
http://www.unesco.org/most/brochur3.htm

Interactive Guide to the Internet
http://www.sierramm.com/smpnet.html

Evaluating Internet Resources
http://www.albany.edu/library/internet/evaluate.html

Evaluating Quality on the Net
http://www.tiac.net/users/hope/findqual.html

Digital Library Websites

Gateway to Europe's National Libraries
http://portico.bl.uk/gabriel/

Worldwide Digital Library Research Projects
http://www.dlib.org/projects.html#national

Digital Library Initiative (Social Science Team)
http://anshar.grainger.uiuc.edu/dlisoc/socsci_site/index.html

University of California at Berkeley
http://elib.cs.berkeley.edu/

University of Michigan
http://www.si.umich.edu/UMDL

University of Illinois
http://dli.grainger.uiuc.edu

University of California at Santa Barbara
http://alexandria.sdc.ucsb.edu/

Carnegie Mellon University
http://www.informedia.cs.cmu.edu

Library of Congress Digital Library
http://www.loc.gov/

Berkeley Digital Library SunSITE
http://sunsite.berkeley.edu/

Humanities Texts
http://english-server.hss.cmu.edu

eLib Homepage
http://ukoln.bath.ac.uk/elib/

The Electric Library
http://www.elibrary.com/

The Electronic Newsstand
http://www.enews.com

General Websites for Humanities and Social Sciences

The HUMBUL Gateway: International Resources for the Humanities
http://users.ox.ac.uk/~humbul/

Humanities HUB: Selected Resources for the Social Sciences
and Humanities
http://www.gu.edu.au/gwis/hub/

TradeWave Galaxy: Humanities/Social Sciences Indices
http://www.einet.net

Social Science Indices
http://www.osu.edu/units/sociology/indices.htm

Coombsweb Social Sciences Server
http://coombs.anu.edu.au/

INFOMINE for the Social Sciences, Humanities, and the Arts.
http://lib-www.ucr.edu/liberal/

The Argus Clearinghouse: Arts and Humanities/Social Sciences and Social Issues
http://www.clearinghouse.net/index.html

The WWW Virtual Library
http://vlib.stanford.edu/Overview.html

Voice of the Shuttle Guide to the Humanities and Social Sciences
http://humanitas.ucsb.edu/

H-Net: Humanities and Social Sciences Online Home Page
http://h-net.msu.edu/

Social Science Information Gateway
http://sosig.ac.uk/

Forum on Technology, Media and Society
http://tunisia.sdc.ucsb.edu/speed/

References

Webster's Dictionary
http://work.ucsd.edu:5141/cgi-bin/http_webster

The Semantic Rhyming Dictionary
http://www.link.cs.cmu.edu/dougb/rhyme-doc.html

ROGET'S Thesaurus Search Form
http://humanities.uchicago.edu/forms_unrest/ROGET.html

Strunk and White's Elements of Style
http://www.columbia.edu/acis/bartleby/strunk/

Acronym and Abbreviation List
http://www.ucc.ie/info/net/acronyms/

Shakespeare Glossary
http://english-www.hss.cmu.edu/langs/shakespeare-glossary.txt

An Elementary Grammar
http://vweb1.hiway.co.uk/ei/intro.html

Punctuation
http://aix1.uottawa.ca/academic/arts/writcent/hypergrammar/punct.html

Rhetoric and Composition

Rhetoric and Composition
http://eserver.org/rhetoric/

A Glossary of Rhetorical Terms
http://www.uky.edu/ArtsSciences/Classics/rhetoric.html

Composition & Rhetoric Bibliographic Database
http://www.public.iastate.edu/~honeyl/bib/index.html

World-Wide Web Resources for Rhetoric and Composition
http://www.ihets.org/information/internet/comp.html

Classical Rhetoric

The Forest of Rhetoric
http://humanities.byu.edu/rhetoric/forest.htm

School of Classics Networked Resources in Classics
http://www.leeds.ac.uk/classics/resources/index.html#Teaching

Rhetoric
http://www.tdandw.com/rhetoric.htm

Classics

The Library of Congress Resources for Greek and Latin Classics
http://lcweb.loc.gov/global/classics/classics.html

Greek Mythology Link
http://hsa.brown.edu/~maicar/

Bullfinch's Mythology
http://www.webcom.com/shownet/medea/bulfinch/welcome.html

Myths and Legends
http://pubpages.unh.edu/~cbsiren/myth.html

Encyclopedia of Mythology
http://www.pins.co.uk/upages/probertm/myths.htm

Middle English

Geoffrey Chaucer
http://www.luminarium.org/medlit/chaucer.htm
http://www.vmi.edu/~english/chaucer.html

Sir Gawain and the Green Knight
http://sam.acu.edu/academics/res/english/gawain/

Anthology of Middle English Articles and Essays
http://www.luminarium.org/medlit/medessay.htm

Labyrinth Library Middle English Bookcase
http://www.georgetown.edu/labyrinth/library/me/me.html

Corpus of Middle English
http://www.hti.umich.edu/english/mideng/

Anthology of Middle English Literature 1350-1485
http://www.luminarium.org/medlit/

Renaissance and 17th Century
http://humanitas.ucsb.edu/shuttle/eng-ren.html

16th Century Renaissance English Literature 1485-1603
http://www.luminarium.org/renlit/

Electrifying the Renaissance, Hypertext, Literature, and the World
Wide Web
http://humanitas.ucsb.edu/depts/english/coursework/rar/

The Complete Works of William Shakespeare
http://the-tech.mit.edu:80/Shakespeare/works.html

English Literature Early 17th Century 1604-1660
http://www.luminarium.org/sevenlit/

The Bard's Home on the Internet
http://www.bardware.com/bardware/index.html

ArdenNet
http://www.ardenshakespeare.com/main/welcome.html

Mr. William Shakespeare and the Internet
http://daphne.palomar.edu/shakespeare/

Shakespeare Resources
http://www.resourcehelp.com/qsershakes.htm

18th Century

Alexander Pope
http://library.utoronto.ca/www/utel/rp/authors/pope.html

The Rape of the Lock
http://www-unix.oit.umass.edu/~sconstan/

Samuel Johnson
http://andromeda.rutgers.edu/~jlynch/Johnson/

Aphra Behn
http://ernie.bgsu.edu/~smorgan/publick/behn.html

William Congreve
http://ernie.bgsu.edu/~smorgan/publick/congreve.html

Jonathan Swift
http://www.stg.brown.edu/projects/hypertext/landow/
c32/swift/swiftov.html

Gulliver's Travels
http://www.jaffebros.com/lee/gulliver/index.html

William Blake
http://www.aa.net/%7Eurizen/blake2.html
http://world.std.com/%7Ealbright/blake.html

Samuel Coleridge
http://www.lib.virginia.edu/etext/stc/Coleridge/

Lewis Carroll
http://www.lewiscarroll.org/carroll.html

Mary Wollstonecraft
http://www.english.udel.edu/swilson/mws/mws.html

William Wordsworth
http://www.cc.columbia.edu/acis/bartleby/wordsworth/index.html

Thomas Paine
http://www.mediapro.net/cdadesign/paine/

Literature: Victorian Era
http://humanitas.ucsb.edu/shuttle/eng-vict.html

George Eliot
http://www.lang.nagoya-u.ac.jp/~matsuoka/Eliot.html

George Eliot—George Henry Lewes Studies
http://www.personal.psu.edu/faculty/k/a/kaw16/Eliot.htm

Elizabeth Barrett Browning
http://mirrors.org.sg:80/victorian/ebb/ebbioov.html

Sherlockian Page
http://watserv1.uwaterloo.ca/%7Ecredmond/sh.html

T. S. Eliot
http://www.columbia.edu/acis/bartleby/eliot/

W. B. Yeats
http://www.lit.kobe-u.ac.jp/~hishika/yeats.htm

Joseph Conrad
http://www.stfrancis.edu/en/student/kurtzweb/conrad.htm

Virginia Woolf
http://sunsite.unc.edu/cheryb/women/Virginia-Woolf.html

Samuel Beckett
http://www-personal.umich.edu:80/~kadaca/bnormal.html

George Bernard Shaw
http://nobelprizes.com/nobel/literature/1925a.html

Benjamin Franklin
http://nisc8.upenn.edu/AR/men/bf.html

Ralph Waldo Emerson
http://miso.wwa.com/~jej/1emerson.html

Stephen Crane
http://www.cwrl.utexas.edu/~mmaynard/Crane/crane.html

Edgar Allan Poe
http://www.ultranet.com/~rsarkiss/POE.HTM

Walt Whitman
http://jefferson.village.virginia.edu/whitman/

Mark Twain
http://salwen.com/mtcyber.html

Henry David Thoreau
http://www.ecotopia.org:80/ehof/thoreau/links.html

Ralph Ellison
http://www.public.asu.edu/~metro/aflit/ellison/index.html

Ernest Hemingway
http://www.ee.mcgill.ca/~nverever/hem/pindex.html

Arthur Miller
http://blues.fd1.uc.edu/www/amdrama/

J. D. Salinger
http://www.fringeware.com/subcult/J_D_Salinger.html

Wallace Stevens
http://www.wesleyan.edu:80/wstevens/stevens.html

Sylvia Plath
http://educeth.ethz.ch/english/readinglist/plath,sylvia.html

Robert Frost
http://144.96.211.125/frost/index.html

Alice Walker
http://www-engl.cla.umn.edu/lkd/vfg/Authors/AliceWalker

Sites with Multiple English and Research Related Sources

Voice of the Shuttle: English Literature
http://humanitas.ucsb.edu/shuttle/eng-gen.html

Project Gutenberg
http://www.gutenberg.net/

The English Server
http://english-www.hss.cmu.edu/

Rhetoric and Composition links
http://www.writing.org/html/w_rhetoric.htm

Hypertext and Electronic Media
http://humanitas.ucsb.edu/shuttle/techwrit.html

The Online Books Page
http://www.cs.cmu.edu/books.html

The Internet Public Library
http://www.ipl.org/reading/

PROJECT BARTLEBY ARCHIVE
http://www.columbia.edu/acis/bartleby/

Libweb: Library Servers via WWW
http://sunsite.Berkeley.EDU/Libweb/

The Blue Ribbon Campaign
http://www.eff.org/blueribbon.html

Professional Organizations

Alliance for Computers and Writing
http://english.ttu.edu/acw/

Association of Teachers of Technical Writing
http://english.ttu.edu/ATTW/

Conference on College Composition and Communication
http://www.missouri.edu/~cccc/

Modern Language Association: MLA
http://www.mla.org/

Online Journals

Computer-Mediated Communication Magazine
http://www.december.com/cmc/mag/

Kairos: A Journal For Teachers of Writing in Webbed Environments
http://english.ttu.edu/kairos/layers/rebirth.html

RhetNet
http://www.missouri.edu/~rhetnet/

Pre/Text: A Journal of Rhetorical Theory
http://www.pre-text.com/

Inkspot: A Resource for Writers
http://www.inkspot.com/

Shakespeare Magazine
http://www.shakespearemag.com/

Online Writing Labs: OWLs

Networked Writing Environment
http://www.ucet.ufl.edu:80/writing/nwe.html

Purdue's Online Writing Lab
http://owl.english.purdue.edu/

The Dakota State University OWL
http://www.dsu.edu:80/departments/liberal/cola/OWL/

University of Missouri (Columbia) Learning Center's Writing Lab
http://www.missouri.edu/~lcwww/wlhome.html

University of Oregon's WORD
http://darkwing.uoregon.edu/~uocomp/word.html

Lists of Online Writing Labs: OWLs

National Writing Center's Association, and NCTE Assembly
http://departments.colgate.edu/diw/NWCAOWLS.html

Online Writing Centers and Resources
http://www.ume.maine.edu/~wcenter/others.html

Writing Center Services Online
http://owl.english.purdue.edu/owls/writing-labs.html

Evaluating Web Sites

Evaluating Information on the Internet
http://thorplus.lib.purdue.edu/~techman/evaluate.htm

Information Quality WWW Virtual Library
http://www.ciolek.com/WWWVL-InfoQuality.html

Information Quality
http://ils.unc.edu/~fents/310/

Thinking Critically about World Wide Web Resources
**http://www.library.ucla.edu/libraries/college/instruct/web/
critical.htm**

Evaluating Internet Resources
http://www.albany.edu/library/internet/evaluate.html

English Composition/Literature Newsgroups

alt.books.reviews
alt.culture.jollyroger
alt.education
alt.education.email-project
alt.education.research
alt.gothic
alt.journalism
alt.support.learning-disab
bit.listserv.edtech
bit.listserv.literary
misc.writing
misc.writing.screenplays
rec.arts.books
rec.arts.books.children
rec.org.sca
relcom.education
tnn.literature
uk.education.misc

Appendix II
Documenting Your Electronic Sources

Copyright laws came into effect when people started realizing that income could be made by selling their words. In an era dubbed "The Age of Information," knowledge and words are taking on more significance than ever. Laws requiring writers to *document* or give credit to the sources of their information, while evolving, are still in effect.

Various organizations have developed style manuals detailing, among other style matters, how to document sources in their particular disciplines. For writing in English composition and literature, Modern Language Association (MLA) and American Psychological Assocation (APA) guidelines are the most commonly used, but others such as those in *The Chicago Manual of Style* (CMS), are available. Always find out from your instructor what style to use in a specific assignment so that you can follow the appropriate guidelines.

For general information on MLA and APA citations, the best print sources are:

Gibaldi, Joseph. <u>MLA Handbook for Writers of Research Papers</u>. 4th ed. NY: MLA, 1995.

American Psychological Association. <u>Publication Manual of the American Psychological Association</u>. 4th ed. Washington: APA, 1994.

Because the methods of obtaining electronic information are developing so rapidly, printed style manuals have had difficulty in keeping up with the changes and in developing documentation styles for electronic sources. As a result, the most up-to-date information from the MLA and the APA about documenting online sources with URLs can be found on these organizations' Web sites. This Appendix shows you how to credit your electronic sources based on the information there.

When you cite electronic sources, it is vital to type every letter, number, symbol, and space accurately. Any error makes it impossible to retrieve your source. Since electronic sources tend to be transitory, printing a hard copy of your sources will make it easier for you to cite accurately and provide evidence for your documentation. MLA style encloses Internet addresses and URLs (Uniform Resource Locators) in angle brackets < >. If you see them around an address, do not use them as part of the address when you attempt to retrieve the source. APA style does not enclose URLs.

Modern Language Association (MLA) Style Guidelines

These guidelines follow the documentation style authorized by the Modern Language Association for electronic sources. Web sources are documented in basically the same way as traditional sources. According to the MLA Web site, the following items should be included if they are available:

1. Name of the author, editor, compiler, or translator of the source (if available and relevant), reversed for alphabetizing and followed by an abbreviation, such as *ed.*, if appropriate
2. Title of a poem, short story, article, or similar short work within a scholarly project, database, or periodical (in quotation marks); or title of a posting to a discussion list or forum (taken from the subject line and put in quotation marks), followed by the description *Online posting*
3. Title of a book (underlined)
4. Name of the editor, compiler, or translator of the text (if relevant and if not cited earlier), preceded by the appropriate abbreviation, such as *ed.*
5. Publication information for any print version of the source
6. Title of the scholarly project, database, periodical, or professional or personal site (underlined); or, for a professional or personal site with no title, a description such as *Home page*
7. Name of the editor of the scholarly project or database (if available)
8. Version number of the source (if not part of the title) or, for a journal, the volume number, issue number, or other identifying number
9. Date of electronic publication, of the latest update, or of posting

10. For a posting to a discussion list or forum, the name of the list or forum
11. The number range or total number of pages, paragraphs, or other sections, if they are numbered
12. Name of any institution or organization sponsoring or associated with the Web site
13. Date when the researcher accessed the source
14. Electronic address, or URL, of the source (in angle brackets)

From the Modern Language Association (MLA) <http://www.mla.org/main.stl.htm>.

Examples:

Book

Shaw, Bernard. Pygmalion. 1912. Bartleby Archive. 6 Mar. 1998
    <http://www.columbia.edu/acis/bartleby/shaw/>.

Poem

Carroll, Lewis. "Jabberwocky." 1872. 6 Mar. 1998.
    <http://www.jabberwocky.com/carroll/jabber/jabberwocky.html>.

Article in a Journal

Rehberger, Dean. "The Censoring of Project #17: Hypertext Bodies
    and Censorship." Kairos 2.2 (Fall 1997): 14 secs. 6 Mar.
    1998 <http://english.ttu.edu/kairos/2.2/index_f.html>.

Article in a Magazine

Viagas, Robert, and David Lefkowitz. "Capeman Closing Mar. 28."
    Playbill 5 Mar. 1998. 6 Mar. 1998 <http://www1.playbill.com/
    cgi-bin/plb/news?cmd=show&code=30763>.

Posting to a Discussion List

Grumman, Bob. "Shakespeare's Literacy." Online posting. 6 Mar.
    1998. Deja News. <humanities.lit.author>.

Scholarly Project

Voice of the Shuttle: Web Page for Humanities Research. Ed. Alan
    Liu. Mar. 1998. U of California Santa Barbara. 8 Mar. 1998
    <http://humanitas.ucsb.edu/>.

Professional Site

The Nobel Foundation Official Website. The Nobel Foundation. 28
    Feb. 1998 <http://www.nobel.se/>.

Personal Site

Thiroux, Emily. Home page. 7 Mar. 1998 <http://academic.csubak.edu/
    home/acadpro/departments/english/engthrx.htmlx>.

Synchronous Communications (such as MOOs, MUDs, and IRCs)

Ghostly Presence. Group Discussion. telnet 16 Mar. 1997
    <moo.du.org:8000/80anon/anonview/1 4036#focus>.

Gopher Sites

Banks, Vickie, and Joe Byers. "EDTECH." 18 Mar. 1997
    <gopher://ericyr.syr.edu:70/00/Listservs/EDTECH/README>.

FTP (File Transfer Protocol) Sites

U.S. Supreme Court directory. 6 Mar. 1998 <ftp://ftp.cwru.edu/
    U.S.Supreme.Court/>.

American Psychological Association (APA) Style Guidelines

The most recent (4th) edition of the *Publication Manual of the American
Psychological Association* includes general guidelines for citing electronic
sources, and the APA has published specific examples for documenting
Web sources on its Web page. Go to:

http://www.apa.org/journals/webref.html

In general, document these source as you do traditional sources, giving
credit to the author and including the title and date of publication.
Include as much information as possible to help your reader to be able
to retrieve the information. Any sources that are not generally available
to your readers should be documented within the body of your writing
as a personal communication but not included in your reference list.
Such sources include material from listservs, newsgroups, Internet relay
chats (IRCs), MOOs, MUDs, and e-mail.

According to information at the Web site for the American Psychological Association entitled "How to Cite Information From the World
Wide Web"*

All references begin with the same information that would be provided for a printed source (or as much of that information as possible). The Web information is then placed at the end of the reference. It is important to use the "Retrieved from" and the date because documents on the Web may change in content, move, or be removed from a site altogether. . . . To cite a Web site in text (but not a specific document), it's sufficient to give the address (e.g., http://www.apa.org) there. No reference entry is needed.

*http://www.apa.org/journals/webref.html

Use the following guidelines to include a source in your reference list:

```
Name of author [if given]. (Publication date) [in
parentheses]. Title of the article [following APA guidelines
for capitalization]. Title of periodical or electronic text
[underlined]. Volume number and/or pages [if any]. Retrieved
[include the date here] from the World Wide Web: [include the
URL here, and do not end with a period]
```

Examples:

Journal Article

```
Fine, M. A. & Kurdek, L. A. (1993, November). Reflections
on determining authorship credit and authorship order on
faculty-student collaborations. American Psychologist, 48.11,
1141-1147. Retrieved March 6, 1998 from the World Wide Web:
http://www.apa.org/journals/amp/kurdek.html
```

Newspaper Article

```
Murray, B. (1998, February). Email bonding with your
students. APA Monitor [Newspaper, selected stories on line].
Retrieved March 6, 1998 from the World Wide Web:
http://www.apa.org/
monitor/bond.html
```

Appendix III
Evaluating Online Sources
Look Before You Link—URLs

The books and periodicals that you access in a college library are organized and screened for reliability by librarians. But what if you are looking for information on the World Wide Web? The Web is a great place to find information, but the information is not organized, and the sources of information are not always credible or useful. Anyone with a little server space can put out information or misinformation. It is essential, then, to learn how to access and screen materials you find on the Web to ensure that you are, in fact, accessing accurate data.

How do you discern reliable and unreliable sources on the Internet? And more specifically, how do you know which sources would be best to use in a research paper or essay? Before you visit a site, there are some ways of evaluating its usefulness for your purpose. As you peruse the links listed on your search results page, try to eliminate sites *before* you visit them.

First, you should be very clear as to your teacher's instructions regarding acceptable and unacceptable sources. If your instructor is familiar with the Web, then she will probably have some guidelines for you to follow. For example, she might stipulate that for this project you may not use personal home pages or that you may not use sites sponsored by advocacy organizations, although perhaps those sources would be valid for a different kind of project. Second, you will need to have a clear focus of the nature of your project, for that will determine the types of sources that you will use.

Although not a sure-fire way to check the validity of a source, a trick to help you sift through the results page of a Web query is to check the URL (Uniform Resource Locator) for information about the site's source. Each URL has a couple of basic parts just like a residential address. Think of it as a postal address strung together without any spaces. The three main components of a URL are the **protocol**, the **domain**, and the **path**. Sometimes the **file type** is indicated as well. The protocol of the URL indicates how the information is stored. The most common protocol you will be working with in a Web search is **http** (hypertext transfer protocol), but you might also encounter **gopher** (a menu file retrieval service), **telnet** (to log on to a remote computer) and **ftp** (file transfer protocol) sources as well. Not too long ago, you would have needed a separate program to access gopher, ftp, and sites with other protocols; now you can access most of them with your Web browser.

The domain indicates the organization, and the domain suffix indicates the type of organization. In the near future, domain names will probably expand and change to accommodate increased Web size. For now, the most common domain endings are *.gov, .com, .org, .net,* and *.edu.* Domain names that end in *.gov* are government sites; *.org* sites are nonprofit organizations; *.com* and *.net* usually indicate commercial sites or sites that support personal home pages; *.edu* indicates educational sites. You can tell a lot about a site before you visit it, then, just by looking at the domain.

Don't just trust or mistrust a site, though, because it has a particular domain name. Just because a URL has *.edu* in it doesn't necessarily make it a valid research source. You might find student hypertext projects or student home pages that might provide you with helpful links to scholarly or credible sources, but you won't want to use a student home page as a source in your research paper. On the other hand, don't mistrust a *.com* site just because it is commercial. Look at the domain for this address, for example. Many commercial sites are devoted to communicating pertinent and important information to the public. But looking before you link is a good way to avoid frustration as you search for information.

The path indicates the location of the Web page on the server. It is possible that the file name and type will be indicated as well. To put it all together, examine the following URL:

http://www.blinncol.edu/disted/tips.html

HTTP indicates the language (hypertext), blinncol.edu is the domain name (an educational site), the path or part of the server that hosts the file is disted, and the file name is tips. The .html extension indicates that this file is a Web page.

Glossary
Fasten Your Seatbelts
Jargon to Go

And a technological extension of our bodies designed to alleviate physical stress can bring on psychic stress that may be much worse.

ActiveX   This is a resource developed by Microsoft to extend the function of their *Internet Explorer* software.

Archie   This is a search tool used to find resources that are stored on Internet-based FTP servers. Archie is short for Archive because it performs an archive search for resources. (See *FTP* and *Server*.)

AVI   This stands for Audio/Video Interleaved. It is a Microsoft Corporation format for encoding video and audio for digital transmission.

Background   This refers to an image or color that is present in the background of a viewed Web document. Complex images are becoming very popular as backgrounds but require a great deal more time to download. The color of the default background can be set for most Web browsers.

Bookmark   This refers to a list of URLs saved within a browser. The user can edit and modify the bookmark list to add and delete URLs as the user's interests change. *Bookmark* is a term used by Netscape to refer to the user's list of URLs; *Hotlist* is used in *Mosaic* for the same purpose. (See *Hotlist*, *Mosaic*, and *URL*.)

Browser   This is a software program that is used to view and browse information on the Internet. Browsers are also referred to as clients. (See *Client*.)

Bulletin Board Service This is an electronic bulletin board. It is sometimes referred to as a BBS. Information on a BBS is posted to a computer where people can access, read, and comment on it. A BBS may or may not be connected to the Internet. Some are accessible by modem dial-in only.

Cache This refers to a section of memory that is set aside to store information that is frequently used by the computer . Most browsers will create a cache for commonly accessed images. An example might be the images appearing in the user's homepage. Retrieving images from the cache is much quicker than downloading the images from the original source each time they are required.

Chat room This is a site that allows real-time, person-to-person interactions.

Clickable image (Clickable map) This refers to an interface used in Web documents that allow the user to click, or select, different areas of an image and receive different responses. Clickable images are becoming a popular way to offer a user many different selections within a common visual format.

Client This is a software program used to view information from remote computers. Clients function in a Client-Server information exchange model. This term may also be loosely applied to the computer that is used to request information from the server. (See *Server*.)

Compressed file This refers to a file or document that has been compacted to save memory space so that it can be easily and quickly transferred through the Internet.

Download This is the process of transferring a file, document, or program from a remote computer to a local computer. (See *Upload*.)

E-mail This is the short name for electronic mail. E-mail is sent electronically from one person to one or many other people. Some companies have e-mail systems that are not part of the Internet.

FAQ This stands for Frequently Asked Questions. A FAQ is a file or document in which a moderator or administrator will post commonly asked questions and their answers. If you have a question, you should check for the answer in a FAQ first.

Forms This refers to an interface element used within Web documents to allow the user to send information back to a Web server. With a forms interface, the user is requested to type responses within entry windows to be returned to the server for processing. Forms rely on a server computer to process the submittals. They are becoming more common as browser and server software improve.

FTP This stands for *File Transfer Protocol*. It is a procedure used to transfer large files and programs from one computer to another. Access to the computer to transfer files may or may not require a password. Some FTP servers are set up to allow public access by anonymous log-on. This process is referred to as *Anonymous FTP*.

GIF This stands for Graphics Interchange Format. It is a format created by CompuServe to allow electronic transfer of digital images. GIF files are a commonly-used format and can be viewed by both *Macintosh* and *Windows* users.

Gopher This is a format structure and resource for providing information on the Internet. It was created at the University of Minnesota

GUI This is an acronym for Graphical User Interface. It is a combination of the appearance and the method of interacting with a computer. A GUI requires the use of a mouse to select commands on an icon-based monitor. *Macintosh* and *Windows* operating systems use GUIs.

Helper This is software that is used to help a browser view information formats that it couldn't normally view.

Homepage This refers to a Web document that a browser loads as a point of departure to browse the Internet. It also refers to a Web page maintained by an individual. In the most general sense, it is used to refer to any Web document.

Hotlist   This is a list of URLs saved within the *Mosaic* Web browser. This same list is referred to as a *Bookmark* within the Netscape Web browser.

HTML   An abbreviation for HyperText Markup Language, the common language used to write documents that appear on the World Wide Web.

HTTP   An abbreviation for HyperText Transport Protocol, the common protocol used to communicate between World Wide Web servers.

Hypertext   This refers to text elements within a document that have an embedded connection to another item. Web documents use hypertext links to access documents, images, sounds, and video files from the Internet.

Inline image   This refers to images that are viewed along with text on Web documents. All inline images are in the GIF format. JPEG format is the other common image format for Web documents; an external viewer is typically required to view JPEG documents.

Java   This is an object-oriented programming language developed by Sun Microsystems.

JavaScript   This is a scripting language developed by Netscape in cooperation with Sun Microsystems to add functionality to the basic Web page. It is not as powerful as *Java* and works primarily from the client side.

JPEG   This stands for Joint Photographic Experts Group. It is also commonly used to refer to a format used to transfer digital images. (See *Inline image.*)

Jughead   This is a service for performing searches on the Internet. (See *Archie* and *VERONICA*.)

Mosaic   This is the name of the browser that was created at the National Center for Supercomputing Applications. It was the first Web browser to have a consistent interface for the Macintosh, Windows, and UNIX environments. The success of this browser is responsible for the expansion of the Web.

MPEG   This stands for Motion Picture Experts Group. It is also a format used to make, view, and transfer both digital audio and digital video files.

Newsgroup   This is the name for the discussion groups that can be on the *Usenet*. Not all newsgroups are accessible through the Internet. Some are accessible only through a modem connection. (See *Usenet*.)

Plug-in   This is a resource that is added to the Netscape *Navigator* to extend its basic function.

QuickTime   This is a format used by Apple Computer to make, view, edit, and send digital audio and video.

Server   This is a software program used to provide or serve information to remote computers. Servers function in a Client-Server information exchange model. This term may also be loosely applied to the computer that is used to serve the information. (See *Client*.)

Table   This refers to a specific formatting element found in HTML pages. Tables are used on HTML documents to visually organize information.

Telnet   This is the process of remotely connecting and using a computer at a distant location.

Upload   This is the process of moving or transferring a document, file, or program from one computer to another computer.

URL   This is an abbreviation for Universal Resource Locator. It is an address used by people on the Internet to locate documents. URLs specify the protocol for information transfer, the host computer address, the path to the desired file, and the name of the file requested.

Usenet   This is a world-wide system of discussion groups, also called newsgroups. There are many thousands of newsgroups, but only a percentage of these are accessible from the Internet.

VERONICA   This stands for *Very Easy Rodent-Oriented Netwide Index to Computerized Archives*. This is a database of menu names from a large number of Gopher servers. It is a quick and easy way to search Gopher resources for information by keyword. It was developed at the University of Nevada.

VRML   This stands for Virtual Reality Markup Language. It was developed to allow the creation of virtual reality worlds. Your browser may need a specific plug-in to view VRML pages.

WAIS   This stands for Wide Area Information Servers. This is a software package that allows the searching of large indices of information on the Internet.

WAV   This stands for Waveform sound format. It is a Microsoft Corporation format for encoding sound files.

Web (WWW)   This stands for the World Wide Web. When loosely applied, this term refers to the Internet and all of its associated elements, including Gopher, FTP, HTTP, and others. More specifically, this term refers to a subset of the servers on the Internet that use HTTP to transfer hyperlinked document in a page-like format.

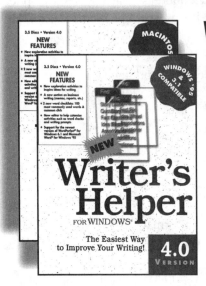